D1547608

All things LBI

FAVES · HISTORY · LEGENDS · LORE

RAY FISK AND LESLEE GANSS

DOWN THE SHORE
PUBLISHING
West Creek, New Jersey

For Noah.

Down The Shore Publishing Corp
Box 100, West Creek, N.J. 08092
www.down-the-shore.com

The words "Down The Shore" and the Down The Shore Publishing logo
are registered U.S. Trademarks.

Printed in China
4 6 8 10 9 7 5 3
3rd Printing, with revisions, 2022

Cover and book design: Leslee Ganss.

Library of Congress Cataloging-in-Publication Data

Names: Fisk, Ray, 1957- author. | Ganss, L. (Leslee), 1958- author.
Title: All things LBI : faves, history, legends, lore / by Ray Fisk and
Leslee Ganss.
Other titles: All things Long Beach Island
Description: West Creek, NJ : Down The Shore Publishing, 2016.
Identifiers: LCCN 2016012428 | ISBN 9781593221065
Subjects: LCSH: Long Beach Island (N.J.)--History. | Long Beach Island
(N.J.)--Social life and customs. | Seaside resorts--New Jersey--Long Beach
Island.
Classification: LCC F142.L65 F57 2016 | DDC 974.9/48--dc23
LC record available at http://lccn.loc.gov/2016012428
978-1-59322-106-5

Contents

Seaside dragonlet landing.

Sandpipers take flight.

Preface

"All" is an exaggeration.

There can never be a complete "all things Long Beach Island" because it's an idea that's always being conceived in new ways, always being added to, always freshly discovered. (And re-discovered.) "All" is impossible. There is no limit. *Infinite Things LBI* would have been a more accurate title. Yet while this book may not include everything LBI, all things here truly are LBI.

So many different things to so many people, Long Beach Island is both a collective experience and a very personal one. It's more than just a physical place. It's a spiritual home and it's unique to each of us.

The LBI you perceive is different from the LBI in anyone else's mind. It's imaginative, too: The Island is often what people want it to be regardless of the reality. Is it the "Hamptons, south," as some would

have you believe, an exclusive enclave of the 1%? Or is it the laid-back summer hang-out for generations of families who return to the same cedar-shake Cape Cod with that funky outside shower and sand in the sheets? Is it a quaint fishing community? Is it the anti-boardwalk resort? Is it a retirement community, or a youthful, music-filled, nightclub experience? Or is it all the above, but still about the simple things — fishing, sailing, surfing, lying on the beach? There are groupings — summer/off-season, tourists/residents, young, old, families; there are neighborhoods; there is the north end and the south end; bayside and oceanside.

We all possess LBI, we lay claim to it. And LBI claims us.

You summered here, you grew up here, you moved away — but you keep coming back. In body or in spirit you always return. It's "things," yes, but LBI is saturated with emotions and feelings. (It's memories of a girl or a boy you met that one summer. It's your salty, sun-drenched childhood.) It's filled with dreams and visions and they won't ever let go.

In the 1960s and '70s, the Chamber of Commerce ran an unabashedly sexist beauty pageant called "Miss Magic Long Beach Island" (there was a spoof of this by *The Beachcomber* in the late '70s, called "Mr. Magic LBI"), but the chamber was on to something — magic.

Magic — LBI has that quality.

The magic, holistic LBI is impossible to fully capture, but in this book we've tried to find common touchstones for our fragile but resilient Jersey Shore sandbar. Well, in our case, perhaps not touchstones — more like beautiful pieces of sea glass or the perfect spiral shell.

Here are shared favorite places, moments, fun facts, and Island legends. We've thrown in some history. You'll find those emotions and feelings here too. And other things that are simply timeless, like the amazing LBI sunsets and sunrises (and moonrises, and clouds, and…).

Partly a list of favorites, part LBI Urban Dictionary, part remember-this nostalgia and history, part dreamlike thoughts and memories, we hope you find your LBI here. Because the best LBI is the one that is inclusive, not exclusive.

We've had to leave some things out and overlooked others. What would you add? What do you love about LBI? At the end of this book, we've included blank pages for your own favorites. Because *we know! we know!* this list is incomplete. It's unfinished. And, most likely, yours will be too.

— *Ray Fisk*

LBI

Let's just start with these three letters. Whether in an oval on a bumper, or spoken in a conversation, or spotted on a T-shirt, they're loaded with meaning, longing, and emotion. They represent more than just a physical place. More than an identity. They are attached to your soul. They represent an idea that centers you, a concept that brings happiness and peace. It's a not-so-secret code — a password that unlocks Island treasures. Wherever you are in the world, if you know what those letters mean, they will transport you and they will connect you.

LBI 101: Come on Over!

A minimalist's fundamentals.

Basic GPS. We've got the north end and south end, as divided by "the circle" in Ship Bottom at the terminus of Route 72. Ship Bottom and Surf City are right there to the right and left, but who says "middle?" We know bayside and oceanside, split for 18 miles by Long Beach Boulevard. But, really, you're not "going down to Barnegat Light" or "up to Beach Haven!" Map-wise, north is "up" and south is "down!" And, of course, it's over to Manahawkin.

The "Circle" isn't very geometrical these days. It's more like an elongated, squashed oval at 8th and 9th streets. But, back in the day, it really was a circle — one of those classic New Jersey traffic circles that have mostly vanished — where then-Route 40 met the boulevard.

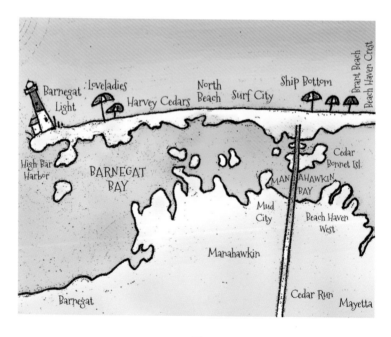

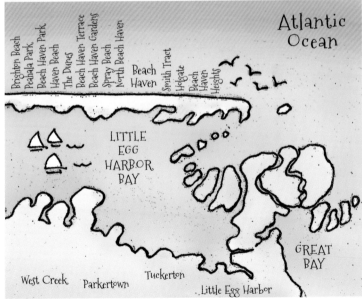

Atlantic Ocean

Brighton Beach
Peahala Park
Beach Haven Park
Haven Beach
The Dunes
Beach Haven Terrace
Beach Haven Gardens
Spray Beach
North Beach Haven
Beach Haven
Smith Tract
Holgate
Beach Haven Heights

LITTLE EGG HARBOR BAY

GREAT BAY

West Creek
Parkertown
Tuckerton
Little Egg Harbor

How quickly the temperature drops as you cross the bridge heading east.

*That first glimpse of a silver ocean
from the top of the Causeway.*

The turning lane: Don't be afraid to use it!

*Pedestrians: In summer, they're
everywhere. It's easy and dangerous
to become distracted. Watch out!*

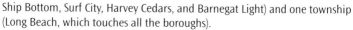

One island, so many towns. On this
island barely half a mile wide, there are six
municipalities: Five boroughs (Beach Haven,
Ship Bottom, Surf City, Harvey Cedars, and Barnegat Light) and one township
(Long Beach, which touches all the boroughs).

And to confuse things: In Long Beach Township, we have neighborhoods:
North Beach Haven, Beach Haven Crest, Beach Haven Gardens, Beach Haven
Terrace, Haven Beach, Spray Beach, Peahala Park, Beach Haven Park, The
Dunes, Holgate, Beach Haven Heights, Brant Beach, North Beach, Loveladies,
and High Bar Harbor. Old maps show more! Don't worry, even longtime locals
don't know where all these places begin and end, exactly. And there's a murky
area where Ship Bottom and Surf City meet; it's not at the Causeway; it's not
even at Division as you would expect. Perhaps only taxpayers know.

It all began with a parade: The opening of the first causeway, June 1914.

Bridge troubles.

The original causeway was made of wood, and gulls loved dropping clams on the planks. The broken shells often punctured primitive automobile tires. Smoke from a locomotive is visible in the distance on the adjacent railroad bridge, which was destroyed in a 1935 storm.

Traffic jam, 1957-version: After three consecutive days of 90-degree temperatures, the open drawbridge expanded so much it couldn't be closed for over an hour.

The Causeway's beloved "String of Pearls." The main span of the Manahawkin Bay Bridge had a unique lighting system, colloquially dubbed the "String of Pearls." It was designed by African-American N.J. DOT engineer Dorland J. Henderson; the causeway was officially named after him in 2000. Before this bridge opened in 1959, an earlier generation used that phrase referring to the sight of lights on the Island when crossing the original wooden causeway at night. The new, 21st century bridge (our third!) alters the visual experience for another few generations with LED illumination.

Summer 2016: Final days of the old causeway (right) and first days of the new (left).

At least today you don't have to pay a toll. You did from 1914 until 1919.

Betwixt and Between: We pass through without much thought, but Cedar Bonnet Island has always been an island unto itself — straddling the bay between Manahawkin and Ship Bottom. This view of CBI looking west shows Charlie Fackler's Bar (on the right) which later became the Dutchman's. Van's bar, on the left, became Eddie's Causeway Inn and was torn down when the Causeway was built in the late '50s.

Ashley Vosseller

The last inhabitants party at the end of an era in 1979.

The Shack on the Causeway (RIP). After the lighthouse, and the *Lucy Evelyn* (lost to fire in 1972), the Shack was probably LBI's most iconic structure until it floated away in Superstorm Sandy. Originally the "Happy Days Gunning Club," it greeted everyone as they crossed the Causeway, and nearly everyone felt possessive of it. In the late 1970s, it was rented to free spirits who relished the alternative lifestyle (showering from a rain barrel may have been

the best experience). Parties were held; youthful memories were made, and Labor Day traffic was toasted to. A wall collapsed in 1980, and pleas were later made to "restore" the Shack, or to build a replica, but perhaps it's best seen through the gentle haze of memory.

Ashley Vosseller

"Old Barney"

Old Barney, older Barney, and floating Barney: The first Barnegat Lighthouse, built in 1834, was only 40-feet high. By 1855, nearly six-thousand ships were passing Barnegat Inlet each year and government engineer George Meade oversaw construction of a new lighthouse, comparable to Absecon, the one he built at Atlantic City. (Meade achieved fame commanding Union forces at Gettysburg a decade later.) The new tower — which stands today — was completed in 1859 and had a first-order, rotating Fresnel lens at a focal plane of 165 feet. It was decommissioned in 1944. The Barnegat Lightship, operating eight miles offshore since 1927, continued to signal mariners until 1969.

Barnegat's beam. The five-ton, ten-foot tall Fresnel lens that once topped the lighthouse consists of more than a thousand prisms held together by a massive brass frame; it was built outside of Paris in 1847. The light flashed every 10 seconds for 2.5 seconds, revolving every four minutes, and was so intense it could be seen 30 miles away. But for the curvature of the earth, it could have been seen further. The lens is on display at the Barnegat Light Museum.

"Inlet of the Breakers." The name given by Dutch explorers in 1614, "Barendegat" — Barnegat — because of the treacherous channels and shoals. Henry Hudson noted the inlet in 1609.

Passing through Barnegat Inlet at dusk, a commercial clam boat returns to dock, 1982.

It's either up or down inside the lighthouse.

A maritime forest: South of the lighthouse, you can explore a vestige of the original beach environment on a nature trail that takes visitors over the high natural dunes and through old bayberry, red cedar, holly, black cherry, and sassafras. Avoid the poison ivy that once was everywhere on the undeveloped island!

What a view. If you climb the 217 steps to the top of Barnegat Lighthouse, you'll know the original meaning of awesome. Awe-inspiring views of the entire north end, of Barnegat Inlet and boats headed out to sea, commercial fishermen heading home, and the swirly shoals in the bay. What better place to play "I spy"?

The erosion-damaged Barnegat Lighthouse keeper's house, circa 1920.

The Beach & All That Makes it So

Running to check the water as soon as you put your chair down.

Hopping over baking hot sand on the dune entrance.

Spotting dolphins as they pass your beach.

Determination. Knowing that a west wind in August will bring those evil black flies, but you go to the beach anyway.

Discovering your own footprints in the sand.

Skim boarding.

Surf fishing. Standing in the water, or just lazily watching the line on your rod from a chair.

Spotting a whale.

Those mysterious pods on the beach: A skate egg case, called a "mermaid's purse" (or devil's handbag), once held a tiny skate embryo.

Banner planes. (We always read the message.)

The amazing sky-sculpture of clouds on the horizon.

Beach umbrellas: A kaleidoscope of colors and designs, in groupings or alone, that make your corner of the beach feel like a temporary home. But watch out for the wind so yours doesn't fly off and impale someone!

Little kids in buckets.

Parents holding up a toddler by each hand and flying him over waves.

L.I.T. programs.

Shells galore: mussels, scallops, clams (surf and quahog), whelks (channeled and knobbed), cockles, snail shells, moon snail, slipper shell, limpets, coquinas, sand dollars, jingle shells… Look for them at low tide, or in the wrack lines early in the morning.

Packing up to go home is never as good as packing to get there.

Seeing a thunderstorm looming in the west, but knowing you still have time before it crosses the bay.

Being waved in for going out too far.

Starfish: Technically they are "sea stars," but either name is magical.

SEA STAR
Asterias forbesii

25

Flying kites.

Staying in the ocean so long your lips are blue and the skin on your hands is shriveled.

The guy with white stuff on his nose.

Jellyfish, the stinging bane of August.

Avoiding the badge checker.

Beach Badges!

Which end is up? Digging sand crabs along the surf. (They are really called "sand moles!")

Our three summer gulls: Herring, laughing, and great black-backed. (Please don't feed them. You only encourage thievery.)

By fall, laughing gulls are losing their black heads in addition to their sense of humor.

Informative (names and tides) lifeguards, Beach Haven.

You had to be there: tribal lifeguard ceremony in the late '80s.

Lifeguard tournament: The end-of-summer Island competition.

Lifeguards. They save us all summer. Amen.

Guarding: What a job! Best part— getting paid to sit on the beach. Worse part — the pay.

"Please Don't:" Dive in the ocean head-first; wear aqua socks; wear street shoes and clothes.

Lifeguard wisdom: Whenever a child is reported missing, they will invariably be found having wandered in the direction the wind is blowing.

Piz Buin — standard issue suntan lotion for LBTBP.

SURF'S UP! Jetty Clam Jam, LBI Longboard Classic, Coquina Jam.

New Jersey Surfing Hall of Fame at the Tuckerton Seaport.

Dropping in: The most heinous wave crime.

The various "flavors" of Mr. Zog's Sex Wax — coconut, tropical fruit… Potent aromas. "The Best for Your Stick."

Julie Goldstein: from the book The Sea.

Strong women surfers: Catching the big waves.

Going to check the waves.

"How are the waves?" Sloppy, head-high, overhead, double overhead, glassy, bowling, pulling, wind onshore, wind offshore....

Get Your Lingo On: Stoked! Goofy foot. Grommets and Kooks. Shred. (Don't wipe out.)

Home Break.

Where were the waves? Peckerheads, The Shoals, Coffee Shop, Nunnery, Fish Club (Cumby), Toilet Bowl (Cable Crossing), Tennis Courts, 25th, Shangrila, 7-11, Cop Shop, Shapiro's, The Shallows, Holyoke, Leeward, Silver Sands, Beach 3, Beach 1, Wooden Jetty, Sunken Jetty, Hudson. There's an unwritten code: You get naming rights if you surfed there first. There's another unwritten code that says you may not name the spot.

"Always mo' comin' braddah."

Wave Rivals: Knee boards ("half men") were in the lineup before surfer Tom Morey invented the Boogie board in 1971, which made catching a wave (especially with fins) even easier. (But don't call them spongers!)

More ways to catch a wave: Body surfing is as elemental as it gets: just you and the wave, with nothing between you and the bottom but your suit.

Keeping your bathing suit on in rough surf.

Rip tides.

Driftwood. There's less beach vegetation than in the past, fewer objects are made of wood, and the beach is now raked clean during summer. So finding a gnarly, sculptural piece of driftwood polished satin-smooth is a delight. Take it home.

When the lifeguards leave. That last, short tweet of the whistle, the flags go down, the stand gets hauled up to the dune and you are on your own.

Beach badge collections.

Less is More. The person who shows up on the beach with just a towel and maybe a bottle of sunscreen vs. the family with a caravan of stuff, including tents and coolers.

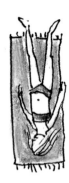

Parental panic. That moment when, finally relaxed, lying in your beach chair, you look around and notice your small child is nowhere in sight.

Getting knocked on your butt and tumbled by a wave.

Realizing you might be in over your head, making it back, and having new respect for the ocean.

Sandbars.

Finding a shell so tiny it's practically a grain of sand.

Sanderlings running in and out of the surf.

Beach chair position: Facing the water or following the sun?

Getting buried. In a more innocent era, before we knew the dangers (and no one with a brain does this today), getting covered in sand and then breaking free was fun for kids of all ages.

No restrooms, no problem. LBI towns do have public accommodations but they're few and far between and not always convenient for beachgoers (a pun). Let's be honest: we all know how the ocean gets used. We accept stuff in the water as a fact of LBI beach life. Number 1 only. The solution, hopefully, is dilution.

Standing in the surf and watching your feet get sucked down in the sand until you can't even move.

"Rules" on the beach entrance sign. How many do you ignore?

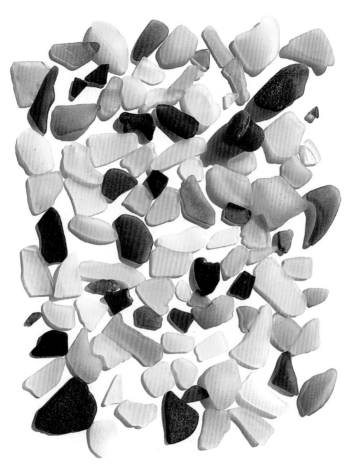

Sea Glass. The only beach trash that is truly a treasure. No other broken and discarded man-made item — given enough time and the elements — is transformed so perfectly into such a precious object. Hunted, collected and displayed, used in jewelry, it's found in a palette of green, rare yellow and red, lilac, blue, white, polished to a satin finish. The sweet irony is that glass itself is made from the silica of sand, and the sand and the sea lovingly return it to its natural state.

Settling in with a good read at the very edge of the continent.

Parasailing. Watching from the beach might be just as much fun.

SPF numbers: 70, 50, 45, 30, 20, 15, 8, 4... Who knew avoiding sunburn would require math?

Even in early Beach Haven, frolicking on the beach was irresistible.

Barnegat Inlet, LBI's north end, the dike, and Island Beach. This image from the 1980s shows erosion around the lighthouse before a new south jetty was constructed.

All Things Bayside

Bays, not just one. From north to south we've got: Barnegat Bay, Manahawkin Bay (under the Causeway), Little Egg Harbor Bay, and Great Bay (off Holgate and Little Egg Inlet).

Blue claws! It's zen and the art of crabbing: Catching blue claws out of the bay on a string line, luring the fierce crustacean to the surface with a greasy chunk of bunker (or, the old favorite, a chicken leg) and swooping under it with a net. How primitive and elemental the act is, and how rewarding.

Traffic: Bayside life is on the water — boats of all sizes, powered by wind and motors, going this way and that.

It's astonishing how long a blue claw crab can live out of water.

Kayaks in a rainbow of colors, sit-on-top or not.

The delight of a natural, un-bulkheaded bay beach.

Renting a small boat for a few hours or a day.

Barnacles: They love your boat! (Immature barnacles look like little sacs of juice — squishy and squirty.)

Marinas: Everyone has their favorite.

Gaff-rigged catboats.

Your favorite sunset spot at the end of the street.

Sunset boat rides with your friends.

In the marsh, fiddler crabs waving that one large claw at you.

Sailing sneakboxes.

Rowing out to one of the little islands in the bay and feeling like an explorer.

Hobie Cats.

Finding a live whelk in your crab trap.

The aerial show performed by hungry barn swallows at sunset.

Water skiing on a glassy bay.

What's SUP? Stand-up paddle boards.

Learning the art of sailing at a yacht club.

Sailboat races: E-scows (left), catboats (above), catamarans, Optis, Sunfish, Lightnings, Mariners, Lasers. (And in the old days: Comets, Moths, Blue Jays, Dusters, sneakboxes.)

Old boats in the yard.

Islands in the bay: Mordecai, Marshelder, Ham, Flat, Clam, Sandy, Harvey Sedges, Vol Sedge...

Great blue herons, snowy and great egrets patiently hunting in impossibly still water.

Jigging for flounder.

Purple martin houses.

Greenhead fly traps.

"The dike" at High Bar Harbor.

Watching the smoke from a distant fire on the Mainland.

Coexist. Power and paddle.

Sharing the bay.

Catching blowfish, sea robins (or a scary oyster cracker!) and the occasional eel.

Bay-combings: Even the shell distribution is different on the west side. Mostly bivalves, there are plenty of well-worn hard clams, bay scallops, oysters, razor clams, horse mussels and — though not a shell — the occasional horseshoe crab.

NO SWIMMING FISHING CRABBING FROM ANY PART OF THIS BRIDGE

Eel grass, washing up in windrows.

The bay beach (or "kiddie beach") — fenced in for your protection!

The fierce bite of a greenhead, and the sweet revenge you feel when you kill it.

Wakeboarding: Making your own waves.

Windsurfing: It took off in the '80s — a precursor to SUPs and kiteboarding.

The reliable garvey, a Barnegat Bay stalwart.

Local ingenuity: "surfing" on towed surfboards behind a work boat in the bay when the waves are flat.

Towns, Legends & Landmarks

Across the Bay: Until the last decade of the 19th century, each section of the Island was part of the municipality across the bay because so few people actually lived here. Tucker's Island and everything south of Holgate belonged to Little Egg Harbor Township; from Beach Haven to Brant Beach it was Eagleswood; all of the barrier beach north to Harvey Cedars was Stafford. Loveladies and the area around the lighthouse was Union (today's Barnegat Township). So if you lived in Beach Haven and had some town business to attend to you'd have to *sail* across the bay to Eagleswood's town hall in "Wes' Crik."

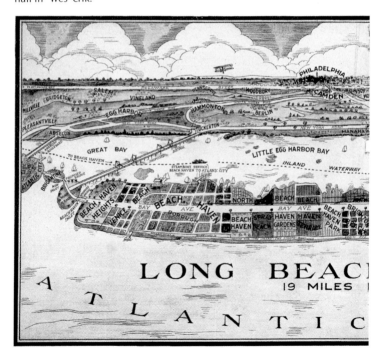

"Sea bathing" near the boardwalk and the Engleside Hotel in Edwardian-era Beach Haven. An aspirational map, below, included plans for north and south bridges at either end of the Island and a bridge to Tuckerton.

The Independent Dock in the 1930s; now Viking Village.

Barnegat Light:
Called Barnegat City until 1948, now it's synonymous with the iconic lighthouse that watches over the town and inlet. Scandinavian fishermen formed the Independent Fishery in 1927 — today's Viking Village. Some of the original "bait-up shacks" are the small shops there today. (Each fisherman, assigned his own shack, used it for baiting long-line gear and storing supplies.) This independent town not only doesn't have mail delivery, it has its own ZIP code!

Loveladies: Sometimes known for its adventurous and contemporary architecture, this section of Long Beach Township was named by the U.S. Lifesaving Service when a local name had to be chosen for the station in that unpopulated area. Thomas Lovelady hunted on his namesake Lovelady's Island, a small island in the bay that has since eroded.

Harvey Cedars is a verbal corruption of "Harvest Cedars" (although a few people still want to think there was a guy named Harvey who possibly lived in a cedar tree). The northern part of town was first called High Point (thus, High Point Vol. Fire Co.) and the two sections merged in 1894. Because of the preservation of the Bible Conference (a former hotel), and Maris Stella, the Sisters of Charity retreat (originally a private estate), Harvey Cedars has the most open space of any town on the Island.

The last of the grand old hotels on the Island, the former Harvey Cedars Hotel, is today the Harvey Cedars Bible Conference. The cupola — the "prayer tower" — was a late addition to the 1848 building. One red cedar remaining on the grounds is a century and a half old.

One of the Harvey Cedars cedars, now gone.

Surf City — the widest part of the Island — was known by various names since colonial times: Great Swamp, Buzby's Place, Old Mansion (after the old hotel, the Mansion of Health) and its first official name, Long Beach City. This borough has the largest year-round population on LBI.

Surf City oceanfront, early in the 20th century.

Ship Bottom: Named after a 1817 ship's grounding, when a woman was saved from the hull, Ship Bottom was originally just a stretch of beach five blocks long. It merged with small developments, part of Long Beach Township, and in 1925 the area was consolidated into Ship Bottom-Beach Arlington. In 1947 the Arlington portion of the name was dropped. The wreck of the *Fortuna* in 1910 reinforced the "ship" reference and this much photographed wreck became the symbol of the borough.

U. S. Coast Guard Station, Ship Bottom-Beach, Arlington, N. J.

Ship Bottom borough workers, including then-Mayor Robert Nissen, right, install the *Fortuna's* anchor, discovered on the beach in 1983 by Carole Bradshaw, seen in the background.

Long Beach Township. How the confusion began: Several parts of the Island were already incorporated towns as early as 1890 — Beach Haven, Surf City, and Barnegat City; Harvey Cedars in 1894 and, lastly, Ship Bottom-Beach Arlington. The scattered parts of the Island that were left became Long Beach Township, formed in 1899.

WATER AND ELECTRIC LIGHT PLANTS.   BRANT BEACH, N. J.

Brant Beach, a neighborhood, began as a carefully planned development on a bay cove where large flocks of brant gathered. It was also the first Island community to have electricity!

At the end of Dock Road, circa 1883, catboats hoist sail near the Beach Haven Yacht Club, above; on the left is Mud Hen Creek, which served as a canal for towing barges at high tide to Bay Ave. The building in the dock view, below, is the old Acme Hotel, today's Ketch.

Dock Road in Beach Haven: Before the railroad and first causeway, this little street was the bustling primary entrance to the Island — via sailboat. Big, beamy catboats with gaff-rigged sails would arrive and depart from the public dock, bringing visitors, building materials, and supplies from mainland towns such as Tuckerton and West Creek.

Onion Domes.

FURNISHED COTTAGES

———

BEACH HAVEN, NEW JERSEY
THE ISLAND RESORT SIX MILES AT SEA

———

PORTIA COTTAGE
Nine Bedrooms, Two Baths

Beach Haven. Conceived as a resort by wealthy Philadelphians, the "Queen City" began to take shape in the 1870s with hotels like the Parry House and Engleside and the Island's only boardwalk. The historic district (included on the National Register) still retains much of the original seaside Edwardian-era character. The borough has its earlier roots in rougher Civil War-era boarding houses in Holgate — the Philadelphia Company House and Captain Bond's Long Beach House.

Public Library, Beach Haven, N. J.

A quiet oasis. The Beach Haven Public Library, built in 1924, was designed to feel like a colonial Pennsylvania farmhouse and has three working fireplaces. The larger LBI Library — part of the Ocean County Library System — is on Central Ave., in Surf City.

May 30, 1949. Opening day festivities.

Schooner *Lucy Evelyn*. It was a real sailing ship — a transport schooner built in Maine in 1917 — that became as much of an attraction as Barnegat Lighthouse. With an idea that the old ship could be transformed into a gift shop to replace "The Sea Chest" on the boardwalk (destroyed in the hurricane of '44) the *Lucy Evelyn* was towed to LBI in 1948. The tall ship was nestled into a dredged berth at today's namesake Schooner's Wharf, and for 23 years owners Nat and Betty Ewer operated the quintessential LBI gift shop. A fire in February 1972 consumed the ship and ended an era.

The lost resort of Tucker's Island.

Little Egg Harbor Lighthouse, still standing on Tucker's Island, top; and falling into the sea in 1927.

The Ghost of Tucker's Island. "In the late forties, along the edge of the deep, new Beach Haven Inlet, flocks of seabirds stood at low tide on a long sand bar, all that was left of what had once been a five-mile island with trees, ponds, a lighthouse, a Coast Guard station, a school, two hotels and a proud little community. It had been New Jersey's first seashore resort. By 1952 even the birds had no place to stand. Tucker's Island had disappeared into history."

— *John Bailey Lloyd, from* Eighteen Miles of History on Long Beach Island.

Shark! Legend has it that the 1916 shark attacks at the Jersey Shore were the inspiration for the book, and subsequent movie, "Jaws." Instead of on Cape Cod, the real attacks began in Beach Haven on July 1st when a visitor at the Engleside Hotel went into the surf after arriving on the afternoon train from Philadelphia. Charles VanSant hemorrhaged to death from the bite to his femoral artery, and the terror at the Shore continued for 11 more days as the shark traveled north to Spring Lake, then Matawan, killing four others.

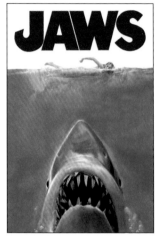

It's possible the book "Jaws" would have never been written if not for the sensational 1916 tragedy at Beach Haven.

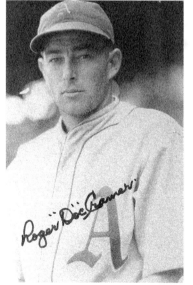

Sandlot of Dreams: Roger "Doc" Cramer was born in Beach Haven and, after he graduated from Barnegat High School, played on the Beach Haven sandlot team (Ocean County Champions 1925, '26, and '27!) Professionally he played (mostly center field) for the Philadelphia Athletics, Boston Red Sox, Washington Senators and finally the Detroit Tigers, where he played in the 1945 World Series. (And now you know who Doc Cramer Blvd. in Manahawkin is named after!)

This really happened. In 1959, desperate to get rid of it, locals dynamited a dead baleen whale that washed up on the beach. It was a mistake. The rotting flesh splattered over two blocks of oceanfront houses.

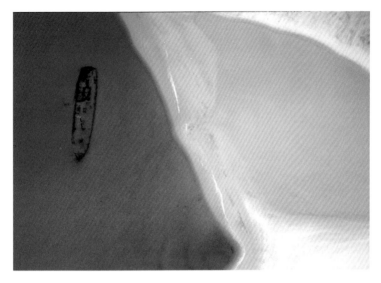

Mast in the beach. The 1963 wreck of the scallop boat *Sea King* is a landmark in Barnegat Light between 11th and 12th streets. Beach replenishment has buried the hull and today the mast stands in the middle of the beach. Other boats grounded near this spot (at left, in the 1980s) until a new south jetty was completed in 1991.

"Bird Sanctuary." The Holgate Unit of the Edwin B. Forsythe National Wildlife Refuge — the wild southern tip of LBI — was saved from development by the Audubon Society. Home to nesting piping plovers, an endangered shorebird, and other wildlife, and forever preserved by the United States, some Islanders still refer to it, not inaccurately, as the "bird sanctuary" or "nature preserve."

The *Hindenburg* over Beach Haven, August, 1936.

Shipwrecks and survivors. In this coastal state, with a rich maritime history that was often overlooked, Deb Whitcraft, former mayor of Beach Haven, turned a personal collection and a lifetime of interest in shipwrecks and maritime disasters into a remarkable museum. The New Jersey Maritime Museum on Dock Road in Beach Haven has an unrivaled collection of N.J. maritime artifacts, documents, and historical ephemera, including the largest collection of material about the ill-fated *Morro Castle* tragedy, which has its own dedicated room.

A giant lens; a small town museum. The Barnegat Light Museum, at 5th and Central, was a one-room schoolhouse from 1903 to 1951. It's packed with artifacts and photos of the town's maritime and commercial fishing history, the Scandinavian families that built what was then known as Barnegat City, and of course the focus: The five-ton, ten-foot tall Fresnel lens that once flashed atop the lighthouse and could be seen as far as the curvature of the earth allowed.

Time travel. Put away your devices and enter the time machine. The Long Beach Island Historical Society's LBI Museum on Engleside Ave. in Beach Haven is an endlessly fascinating treasure trove. From the founding of Beach Haven to Barnegat Lighthouse, from shipwrecks and the U.S. Lifesaving Service (precursor of the Coast Guard) to pound fishing, the lost community of Tucker's Island, the railroad on LBI, sailing and yacht clubs and local boats, you can lose yourself for an entire day here.

Not Just For Kids!

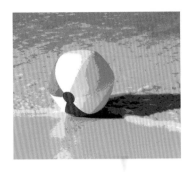

Chasing a wind-blown beach ball.

"Ice cream man! Ice cream man!"

Fantasy Island, what a good name.

Eating sandy sandwiches on the beach and not caring.

Having to wait an agonizing amount of time to go back into the water after lunch "so you don't get cramps."

Primary colors: Buckets, boogie boards, rash guards, "swimmies," shovels, towels, umbrellas, beach chairs.

Festival of the Sea.

LBI FLY International Kite Festival.

The thrill of seeing the ocean for the very first time.

Holding a tiny crab.

Getting to drive the boat!

Miniature Golf: Flamingo, Mr. Tee's Putt & Play, Hartland Golf and Arcade, Island Mini Golf, Sandbar, Sand Trap, Settler's Mill Adventure Golf — you can't miss!

Trying to get warm while wrapped in a beach towel, teeth chattering after an entire afternoon spent in the ocean.

Patriotic holidays at the beach.

Crabbing with your grandfather.

Sandcastles: Dribble or bucket-packed. With or without moat.

I scream, you scream. Frozen custard? Soft ice cream? Jimmies or sprinkles? Whatever you call it, there's always a line at night.

Lifejackets, aka PFDs.

Climbing on the lifeguard stand after the guards leave.

Buying a hermit crab.

Building a super-cool beach fort.

Bobbers.

Mermaids.

Barnegat Pirates.

Standing up on a board for the very first time.

Goal for the day: To catch a wave.

Scary things that wash up.

Finding a baby shark.

Catch-of-the-Day

What is an LBI summer without local seafood?
Clams, oysters, mussels, flounder, mako, swordfish, scallops, tilefish, lobster, crabs, bluefish, tuna…
you can buy it fresh everywhere, or catch your own.

Sheepshead — more popular "back in the day."

Barnegat Light scallops. The boat that brought them is probably right there at the dock. Worth every penny.

Oysters — rediscovered. At the end of the 19th century, oysters were so prolific at the Shore and so commonly served they were the fast food of the region — delicious, cheap and plentiful. Environmentally beneficial, oysters

filter and clean the bay and estuary, so a 21st century resurgence in oystering benefits both our appetites and our waters.

Barnegat Light commercial fishing fleet. Long-liners, scallopers and net boats, there are more than 50 commercial boats in Barnegat Light, with the best names ever: *Olympic Javelin, Relentless, Lindsay-L, Grand Larson III, F. Nelson Blount, Endeavor, Sea Farmer, Miss Maddy, Lucky Thirteen, Gipper, Southern Hunter, Snoopy, John De Wolf, Native Sun, Viking Rose, Francis Anne...*

Bring your fish to the bar! This deepwater fish, an extremely rare bycatch from a commercial trip, was destined for the Smithsonian Institution's collection. It's a bigscale pomfret, just hanging out at Kubel's.

Surf fishing, north end and south end, then and now. Barnegat Light, top left, and the inlet in Holgate, bottom.

Hooked. The "tug is the drug" when it comes to fishing.

Eating what you catch.

Hauling in your first striper of the season.

Striped Bass Derby, now the LBI Surf Fishing Classic. Started by the old Board of Trade in 1954 as a way to extend the summer season, it once attracted thousands with prizes that included new Jeeps. It survived the near-disappearance of striped bass in the '80s and '90s and is still going strong with about 800 entrants.

Annual "Blessing of the Fleet" in Barnegat Light.

The adrenaline rush of hooking a fish and the fight to bring it in.

Fishing in your secret spot.

Captain Lou Puskas, co-founder of Viking Village in Barnegat Light, turned tilefish, a somewhat odd-looking species of underutilized fish, into a modern staple at fish markets and on trendy restaurant tables. But in the 1970s his ambition was just to sell the fish he could catch, and his marketing slogan for the deep-water fish was "poor man's lobster."

A real workboat.

Catch and release.

Fluking with the whole family.

Marlin. White or blue.

Fishing trips. From either end of the Island on head/party boats (*Carolyn Ann III, Miss Barnegat Light, Miss Beach Haven, The Searcher II*...). Or charter your own.

How to clam: Tonging, raking, or treading (above) for *Mercenaria Mercenaria*.

Northern Quahog. The hard clam comes in five sizes — little necks (best for eating raw), middle necks, top necks (Clams Casino!), cherrystones (most versatile — raw, steamed, or chowder), and chowder (the name says it all).

It's all about that bait: Big traps for little fish (top) and millions of surf clams that washed up on the Barnegat Light beach in 1984 (bait-grade only!).

Fishing "The Ridge."

Coolers: The bigger the better.

"The birds are working!" A cry that brings surf fishermen running to the beach.

Getting your fish weighed in at the tackle shop.

Fall striper run.

Bunker run.

Hopkins lure for bluefish.

Grundens.

Independent Dock, Barnegat Light, in 1952. The undeveloped land in the distance would become High Bar Harbor.

Chumming and chunking
for tuna.

A freezer full of bait,
and not much else.

"Killies" — local-speak
for minnows (or "minnies").

Bluefish blitzes.

Fishing from a kayak.

Getting an
anchor to hold.

Chest waders.

Old rods and reels at Andy's at the Light.

Unloading Catch of Tuna Fish. Beach Haven, N. J.

"Got Tuna?!" A 968 lb. tuna from 1939, left, and the Catch-of-the-Week in 1954, right.

Weather, Storms & Shipwrecks

Weather and storms are in our DNA. They're woven into the fabric of our Island lives. They exact an emotional and psychological toll, but also energize us and affirm our existence here. It's man against nature and we know nature always wins. And yet, we stay.

"Storms of the Century." In the last 100 years, LBI has been pummeled by severe coastal storms but not every bad storm deserves this designation (there should only be one). Here are the worst of the worst in the past century: the 1938 hurricane; the "Great Atlantic Hurricane" of 1944 (in the midst of World War II, it was little reported); Carol, Edna and Hazel in the 1950s; the March '62 nor'easter; Hurricane Gloria in 1985; the December '92 nor'easter; and of course Superstorm Sandy in 2012.

March 1962. Some storms are legend, and the March '62 nor'easter — aka "The Ash Wednesday Storm," better known among locals as "The March Storm," or "The '62 Storm" — was the equivalent of Superstorm Sandy, but lasted four days and for five high tides. Stalled offshore, it

was relentless, cutting the Island into pieces. The deepest cuts — new inlets, in fact — were in Harvey Cedars and Holgate, where the sea flowed freely between ocean and bay until the cuts were plugged. Houses floated into the bay, much of the oceanfront was stripped of homes, and vehicles were buried in the sand. Seven islanders died, including the Long Beach Township police chief when the road under his vehicle, in Holgate, vanished into the raging storm waters.

A Navy destroyer under tow broke free and grounded in Holgate during the '62 Storm.

Harvey Cedars after the '62 Storm: oceanfront, above; 79th St. as an inlet, below.

Sink 'r Swim, appropriately named. When the March '62 storm hit, the original Sink 'r Swim shop was located at 79th St. in Harvey Cedars, exactly where the ocean cut through to the bay. The shop and home were destroyed, along with everything the Coyle family owned. But they picked up and relocated to Haven Beach and created a story of Island resilience for another half century.

1944 Hurricane damage: Searching for bodies in Holgate, near Bonds, above, and an oceanfront house in Beach Haven, below. Five Islanders died in the storm. Facing page: scenes from Holgate after Superstorm Sandy in October 2012.

Carl Clark

Superstorm Sandy. It was *the* storm everyone who thought about storms knew one day would come. But it wasn't even a hurricane when it landed and it wasn't a nor'easter stalling out offshore for days. It was an extratropical monster — 1,000 miles in circumference, with the lowest pressure on record — that took an unusual left turn and roared into the coast near Little Egg Inlet just south of Beach Haven.

"Go Away [insert name of current storm here]" hurricane signs hastily painted on boarded up homes and stores.

In storms, we hold close to one another.

Rising on the western horizon, harbinger of a summer thunderstorm, or moving out to sea, the billowing cloudscape of LBI inspires the imagination.

After a summer thunderstorm, the air itself absorbs the pastel hues of the sky.

Crepuscular rays over the bay.

The amazing light show that is a summer thunderstorm at night on LBI.

Groundings still occur. This Canadian sailboat came ashore in Brant Beach in 1986.

Shipwrecks. LBI has been witness to about 500 maritime wrecks both on and off the beach, recorded and attended to by the U.S. Lifesaving station nearest the ship. Seven of the most significant are: the *Powhatan* (1854); the *Elmina* (1884); the *Kraljevica* (1886); the *David H. Tolck* (1878); the *Abiel Abbott* (1903); the *Fortuna* (1910); and the *Sea King* (1963).

A bad winter with ice on the bay transforms docks into serpentine sculpture.

U.S. Lifesaving Stations on LBI, south to north: Bonds, Long Beach (Beach Haven Terrace), Ship Bottom, Harvey Cedars (now the LBI Fishing Club), Loveladies Island, and Barnegat (today's Barnegat Light Borough Hall).

Unknown From the Sea. In one of the most tragic shipwrecks in New Jersey history, the packet ship *Powhatan* grounded in a storm near present-day Surf City on April 15, 1854 — before the formation of the U.S. Lifesaving Service. The ship was carrying German immigrants and all aboard — more than 300 lives — were lost. Bodies washed ashore as far south as Atlantic City. Those recovered on Long Beach Island were buried in many area cemeteries. In 1904 the state erected a monument to "the unknown from the sea" at a common grave at Manahawkin's Baptist church cemetery.

The Powhatan monument at the Baptist church cemetery, Manahawkin.

A tropical storm passing offshore.

The adrenalin-fueled mad scramble at the marinas to pull as many boats out of the water as humanly possible in the face of a hurricane threat.

Hunkering down during a northeaster or hurricane.

Cumulus and nimbus clouds.

Great Storms of the Jersey Shore, by Larry Savadove and Margaret Thomas Buchholz — the "bible" of New Jersey's coastal storm history.

After storms, cool stuff that washes ashore.

And then there's fog season.

Back in the Day...

End-of-summer parties.

Bonfires on the beach.

"The Endless Summer."

Clarence Clemons blew the crowd away at the Ketch in 1982.

Rick's American Cafe. Rick's was host to fantastic music performances on the north end in the '80s. The Barnegat Light venue was previously the Lighthouse Inn, where organist Leroy Lewis also played while the crowd marched around the bar waving flags.

The original Pottery Barge was in Loveladies — and it was a real barge.

Non-Jons: Freedom Surf Shop, Body Language, Rick Surf Shop, and Walter's Surf Shop (later Walter's Bicycles).

Surf Dudes: Brillo, Burpee, Bingo, Horsehead, Huckleberry, Jughead, Spermie, Kenbrah, Twinkletoes, Birdman, Zaney, Surf Cat, Surf Ninja, Doc Teeth, Wooly, Coco, Johnny Longhair, Scrappy Foo.

Doughnuts from Marvel's Market.

"The Tide is In."

Warren Zevon at the Tide, 1986.

Poppa Surf. The godfather of surfing on LBI, Henry "Stretch" Pohl was inducted into the East Coast and the New Jersey Surfing halls of fame.

Nickel beers on ladies night at the Acme.

Trendy drinks through the years:
You tried them, sometimes you liked them. Sometimes, not so much.

Moscow mule
white wine spritzer
Corona and lime wedge
Long Island iced tea
sea breeze
sex on the beach
cosmopolitan
tequila sunrise
rum and coke
frozen daiquiris
(of every fruit imaginable)
piña colada
Cape Cod
kamikaze
B52
fuzzy navel
slippery nipple
mojito
fireball
martini du jour
craft beers

MOSQUITO
1 part tomato juice
1 part vodka
1 part Skin-So-Soft
splash of salt water
Decorate with a miniature back-scratcher!

The HOOK-UP
1 part tequila
1 part whiskey
2 parts Red Bull
Spray AXE deodorant over drink
Serve with speared gerkin or cocktail wienie

The BEACH BUM
1 part Clam juice
1 part rum
2 parts flat soda
rub rim with suntan lotion and dip in sand. SERVE WARM.

Surf City Pharmacy. More than a drugstore, it was where you ran into your neighbors, stayed to chat with Bob and the crew, browsed newspapers and magazines, and never imagined the town without it.

Miss Manners: The old *Beach Haven Times* and *Tuckerton Beacon* were independently-owned by Southern Ocean County's grand dame, Mary Ann Cox. Stepping into the publisher's Manahawkin office in the 1970s was like having an audience with the queen. You were offered tea and pie.

Enough is enough. In the summer of 1987, medical waste, including needles, from New York City was washing onto LBI's beaches, and dying dolphins were stranding. Residents (spearheaded by beloved Southern Regional teacher Michael Lorenzi and others) began a petition drive and postcard campaign expressing outrage. From those early efforts ALO, the Alliance for a Living Ocean, was born.

"Hands Across the Island." Concerns about the ocean's health brought LBI together.

Dolphin die-off. Scores of bottlenose dolphins beached on LBI and along the southern New Jersey Shore during the summer of 1987 (and thousands died in the mid-Atlantic region). This one in Harvey Cedars was rescued by the Marine Mammal Stranding Center.

Bath houses.

Johnny's Beach Wear in Surf City.

Old bobbers, wood and cork.

Beale's and Foodtown.

494 and 492 . A "4-" or a "2-" and four more digits would put you in touch with any Islander, back in the day. (Further back in the day, you'd be familiar with "Hyacinth-4" or "Hyacinth-2")

Harvey Cedars Tavern: Called the Neptune in the 1950s, it was on the boulevard at 80th St., where Neptune Wines and Liquors is today. Neptune Market, at 81st St., is known as "Nooney's," in local vernacular, after one-time owner Joe Nooney who "invented" the not-to-be-missed Nooneyburger!

Lifeguard Ball. Lifeguards from each town would nominate a lovely lady to compete for the title of Miss Long Beach Island.

Who's the fairest at the Lifeguard Ball?

LBI Blues Festival at the Foundation, 1991.

The Pyramid house. In 1980 it was the first house on the Island to list for a million dollars (or a half million dollars, for that matter). Designed by architect Malcolm Wells, it also featured built-in furnishings. A navigational and design landmark on the Loveladies oceanfront, it was demolished in 1999. Former President Nixon vacationed there for a week in the 1980s and was captured in the LBI surf in a page one photo in the New York tabloids.

The Pyramid House
$1,000,000
Available Exclusively Through

HARVEY CEDARS

HILL
ASSOCIATES
J. MICHAEL
REAL ESTATE
494-2300

The Beach Haven boardwalk, above; and the fishing pier in Ship Bottom, below.

Fishing Piers. Once LBI had two ocean piers — one at 20th St. in Ship Bottom (Beach Arlington), the other in Beach Haven at Berkeley Ave. Both were destroyed in the '44 hurricane and never rebuilt.

Emilio Guido's Gateway Bar. Famous for its pizzas — it was the first place on the Island to serve "tomato pies." Guido also owned Ship Bottom's ocean fishing pier. With incredible luck, he sold it the day before the '44 hurricane swept it out to sea.

Long (board) story: Ron DiMenna and Rev. Earl Comfort (first and second from left), with Jon Spodafora, latched onto the California surf craze in '59. Ron and Jon started making and selling surfboards, and when they took a trailer full of them to Ship Bottom they were officially open for business. That's the legend of Ron Jon Surf Shop.

Teenage girls hanging at the lifeguard stand (before there were many female guards).

Seeing the Shack as you came over the bridge.

"Private Property - No Beach Access!" North end beach access issues.

109

The Village Pub. A Beach Haven neighborhood bar, today it's the Marlin. (Remember the brief "Touche" period?) When it closed, the distinctive booths that knew countless Island stories and gossip were moved to Kubel's in Barnegat Light.

Kubel's. In the '50s through the '70s, Kubel's in Barnegat Light was known for having a tolerant and eclectic mix of gays, fishermen and well-heeled north-end elite. As the local watering hole for commercial fishermen, this summer live-and-let-live vibe might have surprised some, but the dance floor was shared as Scandinavian polkas streamed from the jukebox and others played shuffleboard, pool, and darts in a cozy joint at the end of the Island (which it still is).

Sinbad, the Coast Guard mascot, was often served a beer at Kubel's.

Howard's French-fried lobster.

Surf City Hotel was once billed as "The Organ Spot of the World." Leroy Lewis and his big Wurlitzer drew huge summer crowds in the '50s and '60s.

Historical events. In the summer, it's a given — you're on LBI. But the rest of the world doesn't stop, so if you're paying attention, your memory of historical events (say, "Man Walks on Moon," in July) may also be attached to the beach.

The Ship's Wheel Gift Shop and Post Office, Harvey Cedars, N. J.

Ship's Wheel in Harvey Cedars. In the '60s there were Pixie Sticks, Archie Comics and a huge section of art supplies for rainy days! (The elderly man at the check-out took forever.)

Dine in a train car! The Express Restaurant in Ship Bottom.

The Blue Noodle.

Shark scares on the beach after the movie "Jaws" came out in the summer of 1975.

DeFreitas bar in Beach Haven Crest (later to become Kubel's Too) was sometimes known as the "O Bar." It began as the Inlet Inn in Holgate.

The Seagull. Affectionately called the Dirty Bird, this restaurant and bar in Ship Bottom closed in 1975, later became the Bayberry and then the Arlington.

M & M Steam Bar.

Shermat Arcade.

Hartman's Amusements.

"Big Chip!"

Thundering Surf Waterslide: Sanding your skin all the way to the pool.

Locally-sourced. A century ago, the owner of the Engleside, Robert Engle, kept three Guernsey cows in Beach Haven for his "baby dairy" — a marketing strategy for attracting families with children to his hotel.

Ads from the *Beach Haven Times*, April, 1962

Where's Wida? The Brant Beach Hotel was built in the 1920s, and was first named the Ockonickon. We remember it as Wida's. (There was also a Wida's in Barnegat Light.)

Hitchhiking up and down the Island.

The Antlers Bar. *The* college hangout in the 1940s and '50s on Dock Road in Beach Haven by the Acme. Eighty-five cents would get you a big pitcher of beer. And hardly anyone wore shoes.

The Antlers, with cool cats just hanging. "Where do you go to school?"

Acme Hotel. Before today's Bird and Betty's, before the Ketch, it was the Acme, owned by the Tueckmantel family since 1925 — with legends of rumrunners delivering alcohol through a trap door in the floor. Frequented by a hunting and sportfishing crowd and Beach Haven natives, college kids were "as welcome as greenhead flies," wrote historian John Bailey Lloyd. Ernie Tueckmantel sold it in 1959 to Betty and Bird Clutter and it attracted a much larger and younger crowd in the '60s and '70s.

Koseff's — the store, the surf shop and the Greg Noll Surf Team.

Ernie Tueckmantel at the Acme Hotel, in 1981, just before its transition to the Ketch.

Le
GARAGE
PRESENTS
A NIGHT WITH
BRUCE SPRINGSTEEN
Thursday, July 18, 1974 — 10:30 P.M.
Long Beach Island, New Jersey

ADMISSION
$4.00
Per Person

№   219

Pier 18 Mall.

Before his fame as "The Boss," Springsteen played at Le Garage in Spray Beach for a few memorable nights in July, 1974.

Jackie Vee and Paul Presto and the patriotic sing-along at Crane's Surf City Hotel.

Gus and Whitey's in Beach Haven. Owners Gus and Whitey were sons of Gustave Tueckmantel, owner of the Acme Hotel. Next on that location was the Port O' Call; now it is Tucker's Tavern.

Island shuffleboard league tournaments kept many bars open and locals socializing in the winter.

Andy's at the Light: Not just bait and tackle, not only chock-full of souvenirs, they used to have live seahorses in saltwater tanks!

Before Boogie boards: inflatable canvas rafts.

Crate furniture: It may have been in every rental on the Island!

The Incredible Journey: A drink at every bar on the Island; in the end you got a T-shirt bragging "I Survived the Incredible Journey."

Paul's Market in Surf City.

Homemade skimboards.

TGIO parties: You bought a cool, locally designed T-shirt as your "ticket" and went to that year's host bar to celebrate the end of the summer.

Baldwin Hotel, Beach Haven, N. J.

They were huge: The Engleside and the Baldwin in Beach Haven.

Grand old hotels: They're always referred to as "grand!" They were: the Sunset and Oceanic in Barnegat Light, the Mansion of Health in Surf City, the Parry House, Baldwin, Engleside, and Long Beach House in Beach Haven and Holgate, and the only one surviving today: the Harvey Cedars Hotel (now the Bible Conference).

1960: The Baldwin burned to the ground in less than three hours in gale force winds. The blaze could be seen as far as Atlantic City.

Tomato pies at Buckalew's.

"Roving Corn Girls" at the Tide restaurant.

The original "The Original" Ron Jon Surf Shop in the '60s.

The Ginza next to the Colony Theater in Brant Beach.

At the Movies. Once there were three theaters on the Island: The Colony in Brant Beach, Colonial in Beach Haven and the Beach in Peahala Park.

'70s Grooviness: The Bee's Knees, Stop the World, The Ginza, Horizon, Blow Up, Invironment, Navel Base, Underground Boutique, Endless Summer.

A promotional off-shoot of the Lifeguards' Ball, the Chamber of Commerce added the "Magic" to Miss Magic Long Beach Island.

Organized by The Beachcomber, *"Mr. Magic Long Beach Island" was a feminist parody of the "Miss Magic" contest.*

Walt Smith's Garage in Surf City was a hang out for checkers games, and known for its "girlie" calendars.

Skaters outside the bank in Beach Haven.

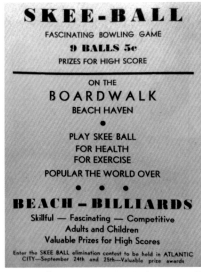

SKEE-BALL
FASCINATING BOWLING GAME
9 BALLS 5c
PRIZES FOR HIGH SCORE

ON THE
BOARDWALK
BEACH HAVEN
●
PLAY SKEE BALL
FOR HEALTH
FOR EXERCISE
POPULAR THE WORLD OVER
● ● ●
BEACH — BILLIARDS
Skillful — Fascinating — Competitive
Adults and Children
Valuable Prizes for High Scores

Enter the SKEE BALL elimination contest to be held in ATLANTIC
CITY—September 24th and 25th—Valuable prize awards

Before the '44 hurricane ended the fun, you could
try your luck on the boardwalk in Beach Haven

Rough Riders: And you thought navigating the Island during summer was challenging: On the marshy bayside, the oldest roads were corduroy cedar planks covered with eelgrass and sand.

Bayview Inn. On the water in Beach Haven, it was the place to go by boat.

Loveladies Dairy Cottage. After you finished your summer art class at the Foundation, you went there for ice cream.

VHS or Beta? A local auto parts store that also rented videos.

MTV on LBI.

"On this island of sun and fun, we never flush after number one." Before sewers arrived on LBI we had clever signs in bathrooms.

Hiding in the dunes from the night "beach patrol" (you could see the lights a mile away) in the '70s.

What am I? Restroom signs like "Gulls and Buoys," "Drakes and Hens" and "Pointers and Setters" sometimes confused people.

Flamin' Harry at the LBI Blues Festival, 1991.

"SHOT TIME!!" with Flamin' Harry.

Hatchcover tables.
Hatches from old ships were purchased in bulk for next to nothing in the '60s and converted into rustic coffee tables. First created by surfing legend "Wimpy" Paulsworth, you could later buy one at Ron Jon's or The Wooden Nickel, resined or not. Unique to the Island.

Bales of hashish washing up in the early 1980s inspired a few clever Halloween costumes.

A&W Root Beer in Beach Haven Crest.

Tee Burger.

Fried flounder at Morrison's, where big picture windows let your mind drift along with the boats on Little Egg Harbor Bay.

The "salad barge" at Starboard Inn.

The Custard Hut.

Star Ship: Locals buying advance tickets to see *The Perfect Storm,* which featured the *Lindsay-L,* a scalloper out of Barnegat Light repurposed to resemble the long-liner *Hannah Boden* in the film.

Tumbletown trampolines in Ship Bottom.

Free Spirit Skateboard Park in Beach Haven.

1982 THEATRE SHOW
SCHEDULE

JUNE 15-21 GUYS & DOLLS

Opens the 33rd Surflight year, with its hard-shelled but soft-centered look at the guys and dolls of Damon Runyon's Broadway world.

This musical tale, relates how Miss Sarah Brown of the Save-a-Soul Mission saves the souls of assorted Times Square riffraff, while in the process of losing her heart to gambler Sky Masterson. A second romance involves Nathan Detroit, the organizer of the oldest established permanent floating crap game in New York, and Miss Adelaide, the featured attraction at the Hot Box nightclub, to whom he has been engaged for 14 years.

JUNE 22-28 "PLAIN & FANCY"

Last performed at Surflight in 1967, the story concerns a young New Yorker and his sophisticated girl friend who drive down to Amish country to sell a piece of property he has inherited, but never seen. In this neighborhood of Bird-in-Hand they find themselves out of their metropolitan world, in a land of quaint customs, stern morals and "Pennsylvania Dutch" English. They run across a romance or two among the younger Amish, and manage to fix things up so that everybody is in love with the right party at the end-- which is how any sensible musical should end.

JUNE 29 JULY 5 "Camelot"
The Great Musical Hit

Opened at the Majestic Theater in New York, December 3, 1960; performed at Surflight in 1965 and 1977, we have here a Broadway and movie legend from Lerner and Loewe. No one need hear the story of King Arthur's Round Table, Lady Guenevere, Sir Lancelot, and the famous knights, without conjuring up dreams of better days, be they past, present or to come.

Love begets tragedy as well as happiness. "Each evening from December to December...think back on all the tales that you remember of Camelot. ...tell it strong and clear, that once there was a fleeting glimpse of glory called Camelot. ...Don't let it be forgot, that once there was a spot, for one brief moment, that was known as Camelot."

JULY 6-12 ANNIE GET YOUR GUN

A diamond-in-the-rough country girl wins her way into Buffalo Bill's Wild West show by proving she's a better shot than the macho star marksman of the troupe. She falls head over heels for him, and he reciprocates until her fantastic feats with a gun become too much for his male ego. He leaves to join a rival show. It takes an evening packed with drama, comedy and hit tunes to finally bring them and their shows together. You'll get no profound message from Annie except perhaps that "You Can't Get A Man With A Gun," but for sure-fire fun, she'll hit the mark for you every time.

JULY 13-19 BYE BYE BIRDIE

The first hit musical about the rock-and-roll craze among teenagers had an original story dealing with the effect of one Conrad Birdie--read Elvis Presley or Conway Twitty--upon the all-American town of Sweet Apple, Ohio. The show, though satirical offers a basically sunny view of modern youth as something of a contrast to *West Side Story*. Among the highlights were "The Telephone Hour," performed in a honeycomb-type setting,a

performed in a honeycomb-type setting, and the challenging madcap dance at a Shriners' convention.

JULY 20-26 ☆ ANY... THING GOES

One of the most successful and durable musicals of the mid-30's was conceived in despair and rewritten in tragedy. The despair was loss of money and poverty, the tragedy, the sinking of the Morro Castle.

The story revolves around nightclub singer Reno Sweeney, her friend Billy Crocker (who stowes aboard to be near Hope Harcourt), and Moon-Face Mooney, alias Rev. Dr. Moon, currently Public Enemy #13.

This show made Ethel Merman a star. This year, it should help another young actress come a few steps closer to her own stardom.

JULY 27 AUG. 2 Pirates of Penzance

Gilbert and Sullivan have been described as the masters of comic opera and the parents of modern musicals. That their works are as much in demand today as they were when written a century ago is ample proof of their evergreen talent.

The pirates in this favorite satire refuse to attack an adversary weaker than they are. The hero is a pirate only because as a child his father told his nurse to have him apprenticed as a pilot. She thought the old boy said "pirate."

A group of pretty young girls stumble on the buccaneers, who insist on marrying them then and there. This is prevented only by the girls' father, a thoroughly modern major general, who swears he's an orphan and needs his daughters. Everyone knows the pirates are all devout orphans....and so it goes--more zany trouble, witty dialogue, twists of the language and clever songs. This continues to the thoroughly delightful ending!

Still playing to full houses on Broadway, in its current run, we are delighted to offer Pirates at Surflight this year.

Surflight Theatre '82.

Surflight Theater Stars.

The Showplace and the singing waiters and waitresses.

Showtime. The much-loved Surflight Theatre, founded by Joseph P. Hayes, began with an outdoor performance in Beach Haven Crest in 1950, followed by various tent venues, eventually moving to an old garage on Engleside Ave. in Beach Haven. Community support allowed the summer theatre to settle into a new facility at their final Beach Haven location in 1987. After hundreds of shows, entertaining tens of thousands of theater-goers, the non-profit filed for bankruptcy and closed its doors in 2014. But the show must go on! — and in 2017 the stage lights were re-lit and new performances scheduled.

Innerspace Dive Shop and Triton Divers.

Classics. "Island Tribe" and "Winter Crew" and the ironic-iconic crossed-outboards LBI T-shirts by the original Starving Artist gang.

OP clothing in the '80s — cord shorts and polo shirts. Essential and ubiquitous.

Fun with DDT: The "mosquito truck" would drive up and down the streets in the evening; as kids chased the billowing "smoke," adults covered their deck-side cocktails with a napkin.

What happened to the LBI toads? They once were found in every garden.

The Beachcomber. Friday mornings in the summer, from 1950 through the early 1980s, this free weekly newspaper was delivered to every single home on LBI. And it was welcomed! A fat publication filled with great writing, history, entertainment, published by Margaret Thomas "Poochy" Buchholz, it captured the delightful summer spirit of the Island.

A Go-Go bar on LBI: Built in 1929 and known as a very reserved dining establishment, it was transformed by the 1980s when Murph and Shirl's Surf Villa in Surf City featured dancers, including Upside-Down Norma, 300-lb. Donna, and Miss Vicki of Tiny Tim fame. (Tiny Tim also made an appearance.) The weekday go-go lunch buffet attracted crews from every fishing boat that docked in Barnegat Light.

You missed the last train to Philly. The mighty Pennsylvania Railroad built the first bridge across Manahawkin Bay to the Island in 1885 and a railroad line to Beach Haven and Barnegat City (as the north end town was then known). Operated by the Tuckerton Railroad, it carried passengers until 1930 and freight until 1935, when a northeast storm destroyed a mile of the bay trestle and the line was abandoned.

Gathering mussels from the jetties made a more satisfying meal than buying from the fish market.

Ship Bottom Stores, the sister store to Hand's.

The arrival of Bob Schoelkopf, left, of the Marine Mammal Stranding Center means that some unfortunate sea creature is in trouble. Here he recovers a leatherback turtle in Loveladies in 1979.

Vanishing Cape Cods: These lovely and unpretentious Island homes are the polar opposite of McMansions.

"Raised ranches" popped up everywhere the tide surged after the '62 storm.

Jane Law Art Studio and Gallery in Surf City.

Foundation of the Foundation: In 1947 Boris Blai, dean of the Tyler School of Art in Philadelphia and a Harvey Cedars resident, wanted a center on LBI where children could be "encouraged in creative endeavor." Less than two years later, ground was broken on a building designed by architect George Daub that is now the Long Beach Island Foundation of the Arts and Sciences, the LBIF, in Loveladies.

The Frank Lloyd Wright for LBI: Architect George Daub, in the 1930s and '40s, created a handful of homes on the Island that were designed around their environment — and to welcome that environment inside. Graciously unpretentious, open and airy, with large windows and decks, Daub's projects were gently nestled in oceanfront dunes and sensitively located along natural bay fronts between North Beach and Barnegat Light. Several have been demolished to make way for the new, but most remain — vestiges of an era when architectural statements on LBI were quieter and perhaps more self-assured.

Sit-down paddlewheeling: From 1872 until 1886, steamboat service from Tuckerton to the Island was the only alternative to sailing or rowing.

The boats at Funland in Spray Beach.

1970s surf shop T-shirts, with their elaborate designs on the back and tiny logo on the front breast.

Old pilings in the surf. A few stood almost into the new millennium, marking lost landmarks like the Ship Bottom fishing pier and Beach Haven boardwalk.

Sounds of Summer: Drifting from radios on the beach or from local juke boxes, certain songs can bring us back to that perfect beach day.
"Fourth of July, Asbury Park (Sandy)." Bruce Springsteen (1972)
"Surf City," Jan & Dean (1963)
"Summer" by War (1976)
"See You in September," The Happenings (1966)
"Beyond the Sea," Bobby Darin (1959)
"Cruel Summer," Bananarama (1983)
"The Boys Of Summer," Don Henley (1984)
"Summer In The City," The Lovin' Spoonful (1966)
"(Sitting on) the Dock of the Bay," Otis Redding (1968)
"Summer Of '69," Bryan Adams (1985)
"Under the Boardwalk," The Drifters (1964)
"Wipe Out," The Surfaris (1962)
"In The Summertime," Mungo Jerry (1970)
"Sunny Afternoon," The Kinks (1966)
"Summertime," Janis Joplin (1968); Billy Holiday (1936)
"Summertime Blues," Eddie Cochran, 1958
"A Summer Song," Chad & Jeremy, 1958
"Suddenly Last Summer," The Motels (1983)
"Summer Breeze," Seals & Crofts (1972)
"Hot Fun In The Summertime," Sly & The Family Stone (1969)
"Brandy (You're a Fine Girl)," Looking Glass (1972)
(Anything by The Beach Boys)

Reale's diner in Surf City. Seemingly only open in the early morning, bee-hived Fran Reale lined the walls with old photos, including one of her and Frank Sinatra. The jukebox was also a time-machine.

"It's Better in September." That was the 1980s Chamber of Commerce marketing slogan for the off-season. Today it may even be "Better in October."

Boarding Houses: Inexpensive places to stay during the 1950s-'80s while you were a chambermaid or a waiter/waitress and if your parents didn't have a home on the Island. The boarding houses in Beach Haven included Magnolia House and Green Gables (women only) on Centre St., the Pillars on Chatsworth and the Evelyn House (the historic Sherborne Farm) on Liberty; and in Beach Haven Terrace, the Chalfont and the former Coast Guard Station (men only).

John Bailey Lloyd. If there was one person, near the end of the 20th century, who perfectly captured the history and romance of LBI, it had to be author and historian John Bailey Lloyd. His talks in the '80s and '90s at the LBI Historical Museum are legendary; they drew standing room only crowds — with many on the porch craning their necks to hear him. His writing style was poetic, and his three-volume set of LBI pictorial histories are classic works on Jersey Shore history.

They came, they played, or they stayed.

Ray Romano	Frank Sinatra
Jon Stewart	Herbert Hoover
Richard Nixon	Bo Diddley
Tiny Tim	Bruce Springsteen
Robin Quivers	Joe Piscopo
Kitty Carlisle	Jon Bon Jovi
Moss Hart	Chubby Checkers
Elvin Jones	Ray Liotta
Happy The Clown	Warren Zevon

The Cold War spies who built Loveladies. In the 1950s, a new development on the sparsely populated north end was underway; the salt marsh on the bayside was cut into lagoons, dredged, and filled in and Loveladies Harbor was born. But the men behind this very capitalist project — in what today has the air of an enclave for capitalists — were Soviet spies. Lud Ullman and Gregory Silvermaster developed Loveladies, but were also dragged before Congress and grand juries; Ullman fought a Justice Department contempt case all the way to the Supreme Court. After his death in 1993 (Ullman left most of his estate to Southern Ocean County Hospital) intercepted cables declassified by the NSA revealed that the two men were indeed communist spies.

The Main Land

For some visitors, the Mainland is just an area you drive through on your way to the Island. For those who regularly cross the bridge in the summer, it is more than a gateway to LBI; up and down Rt. 9 there are towns historically and culturally connected with the Island. There are bays and creeks, and marshes and sunsets, too, and beautiful old homes once belonging to sea captains. Old-time baymen live there, and sailors, clammers and fisherman still check tides and wind. It's also a place of legends and landmarks. Don't miss it.

Secret hideaways in Mainland creeks.

"The National." Before Beach Haven West was built, when you crossed the Causeway at night the entire area was dark and desolate. In the center of Manahawkin on Rt 9, a block north of Bay Ave, stood the National Hotel. A country band played at the bar there every Saturday night, and the Island crowd referred to it as "Frontier Playhouse," according to John Bailey Lloyd. There was a local group of hard-drinking, hard-working good old boys from up and down Rt. 9. It was an exciting place (there was always a fight or two) — and a very different place than anything over at the beach.

The Jersey Devil. The legend of Mrs. Leeds' thirteenth child lives on — you can "meet" him at the Cranberry Festival in Chatsworth in the fall (or while exploring the Pine Barrens alone... at night).

There once was a bowling alley under Carroll's Caravelle Inn. (There once was a Carroll's! And later a Cranberry Bog!)

Skating rink at old Manahawkin Mart.

Beach Haven West: Many streets named after women...why?

The Bridge to Nowhere in Manahawkin.

Mayo's Halfway House. Roughly "halfway" to the Island if you were coming from Philly.

The Tuckerton Wireless. Rumored to have sent the order to sink the *Lusitania*, its concrete remains can be seen — where else?— on Radio Road in Tuckerton.

131

Manahawkin Airport. A bumpy paved strip cut into the pines and sand hills where Wal-Mart stands today, this old-school airport was the gateway to LBI for general aviation pilots and banner planes. One of the characters frequently seen in the office and hanger in the 1970s was an instructor and retired Pan Am pilot who flew the famed Clipper "Flying Boats."

This long section of pygmy pines along Rt. 72 is still referred to as "the plains."

Be a Piney. The vast and mysterious Pine Barrens is part of 1.1 million acres of the Pinelands National Reserve, covering almost a quarter of New Jersey. The aquifer below it is an irreplaceable source of pure water, and preservation is an on-going battle. From dwarf pines to orchids to blueberries (first developed here in 1916) it is not really so barren. It also has a rich history including colonial industries, forgotten towns, and the Jersey Devil.

Rt. 72 is directly under this Cessna, about to land at Manahawkin Airport in the 1980s.

The drive-in movies on Rt. 72. Hiding friends in the trunk of the car to avoid paying by the head; sitting in beach chairs on top of a van, or watching by the side of road, it was a wonderful thing in the summer. When they started showing adult movies in the 1970s, there was always a line-up of parked cars on the shoulder of Rt. 72.

Catch and release: The county's mosquito commission helicopter became infamous when an errant raccoon was trapped and dropped from the air in the early 1980s.

Mud City, the "town" north of the bridge.

Clayton's Log Cabin. The place to go for dinner in the off-season, on a snowy night when almost everything else on the Island was closed. Small bar, large dining room and cozy

fireplace; it burned to the ground in 1991 and is sorely missed.

Pine Shores Art Association.

Tuckerton Seaport.

"The Decoy Show." The Ocean County Decoy & Gunning Show in Tuckerton has all things fowl and feather, traditional and modern, plus working dogs and puppies!

Lizzie Rose Music Room.

Presti's Italian Kitchen: You ordered the day or morning before and were seated for homemade Italian dinners in the family's well-worn Victorian home on Rt. 9 near the Oxycocus School. You were served a pitcher of wine (homemade), and Mrs. Presti gave the ladies a pack of gum when they finished dinner. Best experienced on a stormy night.

Part of the Landscape: Blacky's Clams on Bay Ave., owned by surfing legend and clammer "Chill" Paul.

Chair house, sit-on-top. Once a water tower near Bond's in Holgate, the "chair house" was moved across the bay to Rt. 9 in West Creek and for more than half a century has been noticed for the straight-backed chair on the peak of the roof. Decades ago, a photo of this unique roadside attraction appeared in *National Geographic*.

Locals, Would-be Locals, & Shoobies

How "local" are you? Stayed here one winter? Worked a summer job in a local restaurant? Moved down from "up north" in the late '90s? Been spending every summer on the very same beach since you were in diapers? Graduated from Southern? Or Pinelands, or Barnegat? (or — from the old original Barnegat High School?!) Or did your grandfather work in the pound fisheries, or does your mother have a Scandinavian maiden name? Are you a Cox, or Cranmer, a Pharo, or Sprague? Did your family have to move off the Island to Tuckerton, West Creek, Manahawkin, or Barnegat because it got too expensive? Everyone has their claim to this sandbar. They're all legit.

Bennie, Shoobie, Tourist. Sometimes just an innocuous description, but the terms can imply differences in attitude, expectations, money, and behavior. Sometimes accurate, not always deserved. There are clueless and arrogant locals — and appropriate names for them too. But, hey, we're all on this island

together. Everybody chill; relax and have a beer and some clams.

Slumming it. In such a good way; being an unpretentious visitor.

The inside joke that there is a "tunnel to Atlantic City" from Holgate, and a "bridge to New York" from Barnegat Light.

Knowing which streets to avoid when the tide's up.

No secrets. There are a million stories on this naked island, and it's a sure bet that what you're doing — or should not be doing — is fodder for gossip and cocktail chatter.

Kinda fake, but it's all good!
1.) Perhaps it creates a feeling that the Island is even more of an island (as in *tropical* island), so there is this idea — cultural imagery, occasional plantings

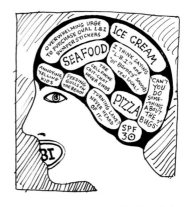

— of palm trees on LBI. 2.) A few refer to the bay as a "sound," which is weird. We have bays in New Jersey. 3.) Those man-made waterways in Loveladies and Beach Haven West — we call them lagoons, not "canals." 4.) "Nor'easter" for northeaster just can't be stopped (it's a pseudo-Yankee affectation — but it's been popularized so much it has to be accepted). It's here to stay. Old-timers still call it a northeaster, or just a big blow.

Those old locals who seem out of place on today's Island, but belong here more than anyone.

High Holy Days of Tourism

MAY ✝ **memorial day** (begins at sundown)

JULY ✗ **July 4th**

SEPTEMBER ✗ **labor day** (day of attonement)

OCTOBER ✗ **chowderfest weekend**

Forever LBI

Embedded in memory, imprinted on your soul, triggered by a scent or the angle of the sun, there are experiences and rituals associated with Long Beach Island — and an LBI summer in particular — that will never leave you.

Bare feet.

Flip-flops lined up on the beach entrance.

Snap shot: A picture of you as a child with your grandparents — or your impossibly young parents — on the beach you've known all your life.

Being lulled to sleep by the sound of the ocean.

"Your" water tower.

Humidity: Your hair's worst enemy.

Polly's Dock in Beach Haven.

Summer love, and your first kiss on the beach.

Watching 4th of July fireworks over the water.

Grilling season.

Community essentials. St. Francis Center and the LBI Foundation of the Arts and Sciences (LBIF).

Seasonal rituals: Ship Bottom Christmas Parade, Annual Seashore Open House Tour, LBI Garden Club Christmas House Tour, Lighthouse Film Festival.

Crazy mailboxes in Loveladies.

Jetties.

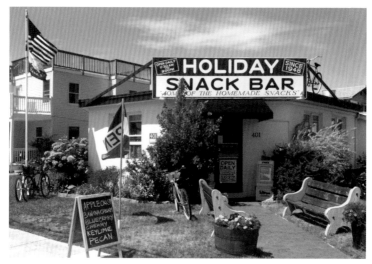

Holiday Snack Bar. What can you say about a place that looks like it's right out of a 1930s movie set, with a well-worn wooden horseshoe counter, cheeseburgers grilling at one end, jars of homemade sweet and sour sauce, old-fashioned cakes and pies, and even a mention by Jon Stewart? It once only employed waiters who were actors at the Surflight; today the kids who work there still seem like they are transported from the 1970s. An authentic, living throwback that's all too rare on a gentrifying island.

Wind chimes.

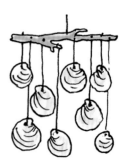

Tender, delicate feet at the beginning of summer. Tough, calloused island feet by Labor Day.

Chowderfest and Merchants Mart in October.

Climbing the Lighthouse.

Wearing your favorite hoodie, salt-infused and familiar, on a cool summer evening.

A contradiction: Even as we profess to value the past on this island, we tear down what is old.

Losing track of time. Having so much fun drinking and dancing with friends that when you leave you're surprised at how late it is, and so you decide to stay up the rest of the night and watch the sun rise on the beach.

Decks. Extended living space where you dry off from a swim, grill and eat, have coffee and watch the sun rise, stay up late with friends, or just have a nap.

The pavilion in Beach Haven

ReClam the Bay: Monuments to saving the quahog.

JeTTY.

Sand in your shoes, sand in your underwear, sand everywhere...

Dune grass. (It holds the Island in place.)

A shooting star over the ocean at night.

Heat lightning.

Exit 63.

The Second Home. It's sometimes called that (more likely "the beach house" or "the Shore house") but it's really *first* in your heart. It's the home where you feel free.

Knotty Pine. The wall covering of choice for a generation of cozy LBI cottages. Unassuming and natural, it can still be found up and down the Island. Preserve it.

Rusty cruiser bikes and tandem bikes.

The old Long Beach Island billboard, hand-built by Daniel Tooker.

Summer jobs: Most seasonal businesses would have a hard time surviving without the influx of vacationing kids willing to wait tables, check badges, guard beaches, and ring up your purchases. From golf shack and amusement ride attendants to bartenders and pizza makers, the army of young summertime workers always feels like one big club.

Putting the boat in for the first time.

Taking the boat out for the winter.

Dune fence. Known elsewhere in North America as "snow fence."

Sailing at night.

Wedding receptions at LBI firehouses.

Cedar Bonnet Island: An Island unto itself — neither mainland nor LBI.

That moment in August when you notice the days are getting shorter.

People meet and marry here: From barefoot weddings on the beach to mayors performing ceremonies, kindred spirits meet on LBI and marry on LBI. When they have children, they bring them here, and the cycle begins again.

The Ferris wheel aglow at night.

Scratching your head and noticing sand in your fingernails.

Pests! You know them by name: Greenheads. Black flies. Mosquitoes. Jellyfish. And the occasional beach badge checker.

Firehouses: The heart of the year-round community.

Only-on-the-Island acoustics. The one-lane road under the Causeway from the Dutchman's to Cedar Bonnet Island and the sound of the highway above. It's always amazing.

Summer friends. "Stop by for a drink." "Wanna go for a boat ride later?" "See you on the beach." Like the first laughing gulls to appear as the Shore warms up, that first seasonal encounter with friends you only see on LBI is reassuring confirmation that all is well in the universe.

Houses on "stilts"! Since the '62 storm, when Island homes with traditional foundations at ground level washed into the sea and the bay, new construction has been on pilings (technically, "piles"). It puts the first floor of living space above flood elevation. Storm surge may wash away everything below (the "breakaway" area), but the house is saved. Yay!

Clam shell driveways.

Saltwater taffy.

The SandPaper. In this era when print media has been declared dead, how many small communities still have a thriving local newspaper with a stable of full-time reporters? LBI does. *The SandPaper* was an upstart when it was launched in the summer of 1976 by four kids fresh out of college; it's proved its mettle through a devastating fire, Superstorm Sandy, economic downturns, and it remains the go-to source for what's happening on LBI year-round.

World-class sunsets. The gem in the jewelry box that is Long Beach Island. Sunsets that leave you breathless. Sunsets that, for a few precious moments, cast a magical light on the landscape, a magic that makes visible the magic that so many residents and visitors feel whenever they arrive or imagine this place.

Sunset on Little Egg Harbor Bay, Long Beach Island, N. J.

The keys to LBI's magnificent sunsets: weather — clouds, movement, and layers — and the wide expanse of the bay providing both expansive vistas and reflected light.

Sunrises: Either get up early or stay up all night — it's equally beautiful.

Dusk. That brief time between sunset and night has a melancholy beauty in summer. The sand and the pavement are still warm, the air is a soft blanket, and the light is fading, gently reminding us that our days are fleeting too.

Living by the tide.

LBI beach sand; the best sand anywhere, period.

Ripples and reflections. How mesmerizing it is to watch reflections of sunlight and clouds undulating on a calm ocean or bay. The only interruptions may be jumping baitfish, a diving bird, or a passing boat, delights in themselves.

Rainbows. Over the ocean, over the bay, over the lighthouse, even over houses and the boulevard — LBI rainbows are extraordinary. They simply stop you in your tracks.

Salt water flooding and local wisdom: You can spot the locals as they slow down and avoid the corrosive water when driving. They're the ones shaking their heads at others who splash through.

Mold on everything, and damp sheets — constant companions at the beach house.

Pebble yards — totally normal, but only here.

The smell of Coppertone.

Clouds. "The Giant," N.C. Wyeth's 1923 painting of anthropomorphic cumulus clouds with six children (including his son, Andrew) looking up in awe, was painted at Beach Haven. The painting hangs at the Westtown School outside Philadelphia.

Driving over the Causeway and opening the windows to smell that briny, salt air.

Garvey races on the bay. Hard-core local boat racing! In Maine, they've got the lobster boat races. Here, it's the garveys and skiffs, two uniquely Barnegat Bay wooden boats, traditionally made both by baymen as workboats (garveys for clamming) and by skilled boat builders for passage through rough inlets and surf (skiffs). The races — loud and fast — are held at various locations on the Island and mainland each summer. It's a throwback to when local men would soup up car engines and rig them in their boats, showing off both mechanical and boat-handling skills.

East Coast Boat Racing Association.

A summer squall races across the bay.

The Clockwork Predictability of a Sea Breeze. On sunny days in spring and summer, sea breezes occur late in the morning. This phenomenon, LBI's natural air conditioner, is due to rising warm air inland drawing cooler air off the ocean. Wonderful on hot summer days, it can keep the Island chilly into late spring. Like the tides, sunrise, and sunset, it is a certainty.

"No shoes, no shirt, no problem." Rarer in the new millennium, but still possible in a few LBI places. As historian John Bailey Lloyd wrote, "In the decades of the '50s and most of the '60s no young person ever wore shoes at the Shore anywhere but to the movies, where they were required or you didn't get in."

A shrine of towels, drying on deck railings.

Riding surreys.

The call of a laughing gull.

That low-tide briny, fertile aroma of the salt marsh and the bay in late summer. It's the essence-of-life smell.

Little Egg Harbor Yacht Club, Beach Haven, N. J.

Yacht clubs.

Running barefoot in the sand. At low tide in wet sand, from jetty to jetty, or for a few miles, a beach run is invigorating like no other. Exfoliation is a bonus.

Sunburn. It feels good and bad at the same time.

Rust. It's real. And it's a metaphor. Nothing metal lasts on this island.

Freckles, sun-kissed hair, and a peeling nose.

"Where is...?" Being asked a local question by a newcomer and giving your best advice — your truest recommendation — and finding this small act of kindness surprisingly satisfying.

The way a summer thunderstorm can pour down and flood Beach Haven and it can be sunny and dry in Ship Bottom. And the other way around.

How a storm will follow an outgoing tide out the inlets.

A baseball game on the AM radio on the beach.

Clam chowder— New England or Manhattan?

Jack Reynolds

The Hudson House. An ID check outside the door on a hidden back street off the beach in North Beach Haven, shuffleboard, darts, a jukebox, beer that's not overpriced, unpretentious tourists and locals mixing it up. First opened as the Waverly Hotel, it is the oldest bar on the Island, and predates Prohibition. It's the Hud and it's awesome and it never changes.

Tan lines, LBI's natural tattoo.

Driving down the boulevard, stopping at a light, and looking over at the car next you just as that perfect stranger looks at you... and smiles.

Running aground.

The taste of salt on your lips.

Skinny dipping at night in a warm ocean.

Skateboarding as a form of transportation.

Why not a single beach badge for the whole island? Like consolidation, it'll probably never happen.

Decorating with treasures you found on the beach or the bay.

Full moon over still water, ripples breaking the reflected column of light.

Beach replenishment: Never ending.

Messages in bottles.

A phosphorescent flash. It's otherworldly: Making sparks by scuffing your feet in the warm sand at night, or watching the bioluminescence in the wake of your boat, or swimming in the bathtub-warm bay — your hands and arms magically creating green flashes in the water.

A brand new book for the beach.

Black Whale boat cruises.

Still Stoked. Growing older and having friends who still talk endlessly about waves and surfing just like they did when they were young.

Trailer parks at the south end. The unpretentious island community.

Generations of a family reunited at the beach.

Local blueberries — Jersey's finest summer fruit. (Cranberries in the fall!)

Riding surreys.

Finding the perfect shell. Whether it's the little coquina, a huge whelk, a mesmerizing spiral, or just a purple, polished piece of surf clam, you can't resist picking it up, taking it with you, far from the beach, putting it on your desk at work or at home to remind you that summer is never far away.

Finding sticky, sandy sunscreen bottles in last summer's beach bag.

Summer constellations.

Outside showers. (Even better at night.)

Pizza. It's everywhere, and it's all pretty good.

The Chegg — often more fun there at 3 a.m. than all night at the bars.

Off-beach foot action. The commemorative Long Beach Island 18-Mile Run, the Dog Day Race in Harvey Cedars, and Walk The Causeway.

Surfers crossing the boulevard, with boards under their arms.

Wearing swimwear under your regular clothes so you don't waste a minute changing.

Picking crabs. Who can resist spending a summer afternoon picking delectable crab meat, making a mess on a table covered with newspapers, the beverage of your choice at hand?

The way that Long Beach Island is a lifelong bond.

Gratitude. Having that emotion fill you as you cross over the dunes, or watch a sunrise or sunset.

Watching the shadows stretch and grow long on the beach and never wanting to leave.

Pulling out that bottle of wine when the lifeguards leave.

Classic. A summer concert at Beach Haven's Bicentennial Park.

Summer concerts. From Sunset Park in Harvey Cedars (No Discipline and Johnny Youth!) to Beach Haven's Bicentennial Park, summer evenings are ripe with free music at LBI parks. Ship Bottom holds events at the boat ramp, Barnegat Light by the bay, Long Beach Township at Bayview Park. And then there are the yacht club concerts.

Oh, Fudge! Lucille's, Country Kettle, and Stutz.

Sweet and succulent Jersey tomatoes. We miss them all winter, and can't wait for the first Jersey beefsteaks to be displayed at produce stands in summer. Then they are everywhere; the uglier and more misshapen the better. Nothing compares.

Farm markets.

Wearing a lobster bib.

White (silver queen) corn on the cob, fingers tasting of butter and salt.

Dogs and burgers — the old stand-by.

Getting religion. When there is fog over the water and a low cloud bank, a sunrise can have a stunningly mystical quality as the light pierces through with warmth and brilliance.

A seawater-soaked neoprene wetsuit, drying on a deck railing.

Waiting in line for a table. For breakfast, or dinner, it's just part of the summer flow.

Summer food aromas. In the evening, if you walk along Bay Avenue in Beach Haven you can't help but notice the tantalizing food smells wafting through the air.

Bonfires with friends.

Perfect autumn days on LBI: Warm water and no crowds — you want to steal every moment because you know it will end too soon.

Flat roofs always littered with clam shells.

History, Naturally...

Not just gulls and shells, not just sand and ocean, there is a colorful and lively natural world in our bays and estuaries teeming with life. If you pause and look, you'll see less common, sometimes threatened treasures in our coastal environment.

A sense of where you are. A century and a half ago, standing anywhere on the Island in the middle of what was to become Long Beach Boulevard, if you looked east you would have seen small mountains of vegetated natural dunes and a wild beach of varying size and patterns, with cuts through the dunes from storms. To the west, you would have viewed expansive salt marshes, and rich, spongy sedge. The entire barrier island was alive with coastal wildlife. And the island's geology itself was "alive," slowly migrating westward.

An aerial of Beach Haven, circa 1930, shows that, even then, most of the Island is still undeveloped salt marsh and tidal pools west of Bay Ave. The train, boardwalk, and Baldwin and Engleside hotels can also be seen.

Dune and beach dynamics: The natural progression for a barrier island like LBI is for it to move inland. Storms move sand toward the bay — overwash — and over time the Island creeps toward the Mainland (while a new island appears, growing out of sandbars offshore). Without LBI's rock jetties, or groins, and frequent beach replenishment oceanfront houses would be standing on pilings in the surf. This photo of Holgate, the southern tip of LBI, was taken shortly after Superstorm Sandy.

Natural dune flora: beach plum, seaside goldenrod, bayberry, rugosa rose, beach pea and poison ivy!

Dunes: Today, the best places on LBI to see dunes naturally created by wind and water are in Barnegat Light and in the Forsythe Refuge in Holgate. In between are artificial sand berms — pumped from the ocean bottom offshore by the U.S. Army Corps of Engineers, trucked in from mainland sand pits and planted with Cape American beach grass. The Island's original natural dunes were long ago leveled for oceanfront homes and views, but the man-made dunes are critical for protection of oceanside property.

Dragonflies: Early summer visitors, their job is to keep the pest population down. (They are greenhead fly predators!) The seaside dragonlet is the only saltwater dragonfly and breeds in the bayside marshes. So numerous in

2010 there were rumors (untrue) that the Ocean County Mosquito Commission released tens of thousands of them as natural insect control!

One, two, three seaside dragonlets.

At the tip of Holgate: A dolphin inside the inlet, above. In 1905, at left, the island's oceanfront was so undeveloped you could pitch a tent in the wild dunes, fish for your dinner, and cook on a driftwood bonfire.

Horseshoe crabs. "Living fossils" that date back more than 450 million years, long before the age of dinosaurs, they are more closely related to spiders. These harmless, primitive creatures gather to mate along the edges of bays in the spring and their tiny eggs are essential food for migrating shorebirds.

"All fluke are flounder but not all flounder are fluke:" This bottom-of-the-bay "flattie," delicious fried or broiled, started life swimming upright. As they moved to the bottom one eye migrated to the other side. Here's the tricky part: Generally, left-side up flounder are flukes, and right-side up flounders are called flounders. More confusion: Flukes are also called "summer flounder," and flounder, or right-side fish, are called "winter flounder."

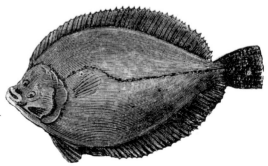

Parents at the nest, left. A fledgling was tagged during a nest survey, right.

Osprey. Also called sea eagle, or fish hawk, this supreme raptor's diet consists almost entirely of fish. Before DDT, New Jersey was home to over 500 active osprey nests. The numbers are now back to historic levels, thanks to the banning of that pesticide and the installation of nesting platforms by groups and individuals who have supported their ongoing recovery, such as Conserve Wildlife Foundation in the Barnegat Bay area. Beachgoers can sometimes see the "dad" dive into the ocean for fish and fly it back — gripped like a rudder, fish head facing forward — to the waiting mom and nestlings on the bay side.

Prickly pear cactus thrives and spreads in many a sandy yard.

Sand patterns, like images from space.

J.B. Kinsey called his eelgrass harvesting business "Kinsey Sea Moss" because moss sounded more appealing than seaweed. Kinsey's nephew, Reynold Thomas, longtime mayor of Harvey Cedars (1955-1985), is on the left in this 1921 photo.

Natural stuffing: A century ago eelgrass and salt hay were harvested from the marshes and bay and sold as material to stuff mattresses, coffins, and car seats in early Fords.

You're swimming in it: Eelgrass, sea lettuce and rockweed.

Meet the *Spartinas*. Two types of marsh grass — smooth cordgrass *(spartina alterniflora)* and salt hay, also known as salt meadow cordgrass *(spartina patens)* — can be found in undisturbed areas of salt marsh. These lush grasses hold the sponge-like sedge in place during storms and shelter marsh life. In late summer salt meadow cordgrass is distinctive for its "cow-licked" appearance — as if large creatures had emerged from the bay to nap on a mint-green bed.

Pretty Crabby. Blue crab or blue claw, its Latin name — *Callinectes sapidus* — means beautiful swimmer. Males are "jimmies," immature females are "sallies," and adult females are "sooks." The gals are easily recognized by their red-tipped claws.

New Jersey has a state shell! It's the knobbed welk.

Swamp rose (hibiscus) on the bayside.

Unlikely visitors: A "local" flock of brown pelicans can sometimes be spotted flying over the ocean like pterodactyls. When the water has been particularly warm, the end of summer also brings the occasional tropical fish that have strayed inshore from the Gulf Stream.

Likely visitors: Harbor seals, pods of bottlenose dolphins, and, recently, humpbacked whales.

The local Lenni-Lenape made "wampum" (sacred shell beads) from whelk shells and the purple inside-edge of the clam shell.

Beach plum in bloom; beach plum jam is a local favorite.

Phragmites: Pretty in photographs, but an indicator of disturbed soil.

Wilderness areas, a hint of what once was. At either end of the Island — the high, vegetated dunes by Barnegat Lighthouse and the stretch of undeveloped beach at the Holgate in the Forsythe Refuge — are the closest thing to the wild and natural LBI seen by native Americans and the first settlers.

Edith Duff Gwinn Gardens. A well-maintained display garden of native plants surrounds the Barnegat Light Museum.

Bay heather is often gathered and sold at local fall festivals.

Salt Marsh. A few marshes remain on LBI but they once covered the entire west side of the Island. These seashore "nurseries" are essential to the health of the coastal environment, and are preserved within the patchwork quilt of the Edwin B. Forsythe National Wildlife Refuge across the bay. The refuge is located along most active flight paths of the Atlantic Flyway, making it an important link in the national network of wildlife refuges.

Serpentine tidal creeks and linear mosquito ditches in the salt marsh, above. Webs in marsh and glasswort (it's edible!) turning autumnal red, left.

A hatchling about to be released into the marsh. Below, female diamondback laying eggs.

Diamondback terrapins. During nesting season these rather large salt marsh turtles emerge from the bay and creeks to lay eggs. Be careful when driving along bay roads between May and August, and if you can, help them cross the road (in the direction they were heading). You may also encounter a terrapin in your crab trap — so check often, as they will drown in them. Project Terrapin helps with habitat, monitoring nests and headstarting hatchlings.

Monarch migration. In October, for a week or two, you'll see monarch butterflies clustered on blooms of seaside goldenrod and settling in on the east side of cedar trees in the evening. It's the annual migration to the mountains of Mexico. And you'll feel sad for the ones hit by cars on the boulevard, unable to take flight. Some local elementary schools have a program where children raise the caterpillars (they eat only milkweed), observe the chrysalis, and attach a tiny tag to the wings before releasing them.

Monarchs warming in morning sun on a cedar branch, and gorging on seaside goldenrod blooms.

No island is an island, ecologically. The environmental health of LBI is inextricably linked to its surroundings. Development and loss of natural areas within the estuaries, on the mainland, and in the watershed far inland have an impact. Storm water runoff from paved surfaces including lawn chemicals, pesticides, even expired medications thrown away, hormones in food, anti-bacterials, and plastics from balloons to microbeads — the ecological insults go on and on — all these things cumulatively affect our marine environment.

Balloons blow: Does this look like a jellyfish to you? It definitely does to turtles and other sea critters. Say "no" to balloons.

"What Do You Do Here All Winter?"

That first week after Labor Day. The weather is always perfect and the Island feels as if it's yours alone.

Blinking Season. Speed limits change and the traffic lights are blinking. Of course there's not much open, so there's that.

The annual Beach Haven Vol. Fire Co. turkey dinner in winter.

The "where-to-eat-lunch?" debate (followed quickly by, "Wait, they're closed").

Having the beach all to yourself.

Arctic sea smoke.

Tree swallows lined up.

Catching the very last rays of the season.

Murmurations: Fall gathering of tree swallows as they move as one across the western sky at sunset.

Crazy people who walk across the frozen bay.

An LBI urban legend: Driving cars across the frozen bay to the Mainland; the proof is in the bottom of the bay.

The day after Labor Day, almost always a picture-perfect late-summer moment, and not a car in sight.

Anyone who has overwintered probably runs half a dozen red lights the first week after they turn the signals back on.

Before there were snowboards, there were duneboards — made in shop class with waxed Formica on the bottom to surf the dunes.

Rules Don't Apply — to some things in the off-season.

Keep off the dunes — except maybe after a snowstorm, in deep winter; locals only.

In winter on the Island, dogs run free on empty beaches and boats deal with ice.

Boating comes to a grinding halt when the bay freezes.

When faced with winter storms, we are resourceful and have our priorities.

Getting around LBI in winter: On a frozen bay, on a snowy boulevard.

Acknowledgments

There would be a lot less "all" in this book if not for the contributions of the following people. What began as a very simple little book took on a life of its own. As it grew we reached out for the talents and LBI memories of others near and far. From reading galleys to offering entries, from suggesting changes and finding errors to providing art and photos (and beach badges), their help and enthusiasm for this project was invaluable.

Heartfelt thanks to our friends (who always have LBI sand in their shoes): Margaret Thomas "Poochy" Buchholz, Bruce Novotny, Steve Warren, Cathy Cush, Jeanette Lloyd, Deb Whitcraft, Scott Mazzella, Trish Craig, Jack Ryan, Gretchen Coyle, Corinne Ruff, Julie Goldstein, Gil Gaul, Ashley Vosseller, Jon Coen, Tricia and Skip Carey, Kevin Carey, Ben Wurst, Jack Reynolds, Merianne Paul Haug, Gail Travers, Gary and Susan McElroy, Linda and Michael Evans, Albert Ganss, Cindy Wood, Tori Hanke, Robert Raimo.

Photo & Art Credits

Down The Shore Publishing archive: 20, 52-53 (map), 58 (top), 63 (top), 64 (all), 65 (all), 90 (top), 92 (both), 93 (both), 109 (top), 110 (top), 112, 114 (bottom), 116 (bottom), 130, 132 (top), 134 (top), **142, 145, 149.**

Collection of Margaret Thomas Buchholz/*The Beachcomber:*** 15 (bottom), 16 (top, handcolored by L.Ganss), 17 (bottom), 22 (top), 37 (bottom), 54 (both), 56 (bottom), 57 (both), 66 (bottom), 74 (bottom), 77 (top), 88 (bottom), 90 (bottom, both), 101 (bottom), 106 (bottom), 110 (bottom), 111, 117 (bottom), 119 (both), 120 (bottom), 133 (bottom), 163.

Courtesy of Jeanette Lloyd, from John Bailey Lloyd's trilogy of books about LBI: 14, 15 (top), 17 (top), 40 (bottom), 53 (top), 58 (bottom), 60, 61 (both), 62 (both), 70, 78 (top), 80 (bottom), 85 (top right), 94 (both), 108 (both), 109 (bottom), 113 (both), 116 (top), 117 (top), 118 (top), 124, 131 (bottom), 132 (bottom) 135 (bottom left), 136, 146 (bottom), 156, 158 (bottom).

Jack Reynolds: 150. **Carl Clark:** 95 (top). **Ashley Vosseller:** 18 (top), 19 (bottom). **Julie Goldstein:** 33. **Albert Ganss:** 81 (top). **Louis Novotny Jr.:** 67 (both). **Trish Craig:** 18 (bottom), 55 (top), 118 (bottom, both). **Patrick and Brian Carey:** 75 (top). **David Scull:** 128.

Leslee Ganss: 2-3, 6, 12-13 (map), 25 (both), 27, 32 (top), 35 (top, bottom right), 38 (bottom), 39, 42 (bottom), 43 (both), 48 (bottom), 49 (bottom), 51 (bottom), 71 (both), 72 (bottom), 73, 75 (bottom right), 89 (top), 96 (bottom),106 (top), 129, 151, 154 (bottom), 155, 159 (top), 160, 161 (all), 164, 169 (bottom).

Ray Fisk: 5, 7, 8, 13 (top), 16 (bottom), 21 (both), 22 (bottom), 23, 24, 26 (top), 28 (both),30 (both), 31 (both), 32 (bottom), 35 (bottom left), 36 (bottom), 37 (top), 40 (top),41, 43 (top), 44 (both), 46, 47 (both), 48 (top), 49 (top), 50 (both), 51 (top), 55 (bottom), 56 (top), 59, 63 (both), 68 (both), 69, 72 (top), 74 (top), 75 (bottom left), 76 (both), 77 (bottom), 78 (bottom), 79 (both), 80 (top) both, 81 (bottom), 82 (both), 83 (top), 84 (both), 85 (top left, bottom), 86 (bottom), 87 (both), 88 (top), 89 (bottom), 91, 95 (bottom), 96 (top), 97, 98 (both), 99, 100 (both), 101 (top), 102, 104 (both), 105, 107 (top), 114 (top), 115, 121, 123, 125, 129, 131 (top), 133 (top), 134 (bottom), 135 (top, bottom right),139 (top), 140, 141 (both), 143, 146 (top), 147, 148, 152, 153, 154 (top), 157, 158 (top), 159 (bottom), 162, 165 (both), 166 (both), 167 (both), 168 (both), 169 (top), 170, 171 (both), 172, 173 (top), 174, 175 (both), 176 (all).

Black & white silver gelatin prints by Ray Fisk, handcolored by Leslee Ganss: 26 (bottom), 29, 34, 82 (top), 83 (bottom), 86 (top),138, 139 (bottom), 173 (bottom).

Too Many Summers, **Artoons by L. Ganss:** 19 (top), 36 (top), 38 (top), 42 (top), 45 (both), 103, 137 (both).

Select Bibliography

For further reading about LBI...

All Things LBI scratches the sandy surface. Almost every subject mentioned here can be found in greater depth in these books by local authors:

John Bailey Lloyd's trilogy of Long Beach Island pictorial histories capture not only historical details, but evoke the spirit of earlier generations. LBI's three foundational books are:
- *Eighteen Miles of History on Long Beach Island*
- *Six Miles At Sea: A Pictorial History of Long Beach Island*
- *Two Centuries of History on Long Beach Island*

John also provided fascinating local context in his introduction to a reissue of the 1906 Victorian novel, *The Tides of Barnegat*, by **F. Hopkinson Smith.**
And he was the centerpiece of three LBI Historical Videos: *Barnegat Lighthouse and Barnegat City; Tuckers Island;* and *Six Miles At Sea.*

Margaret Thomas "Poochy" Buchholz, long-time editor of *The Beachcomber*, a dedicated and passionate researcher, has authored or edited six books about the Island and the Shore:
- *Island Album: Photographs & Memories of Long Beach Island* — an oversize collection of photographs and oral history.
- *The Long Beach Island Reader* — a delightful anthology for the Island.
- *New Jersey Shipwrecks: 350 Years in the Graveyard of the Atlantic* — a large-format history of the most significant wrecks along our shore.
- *Shore Chronicles: Diaries and Travelers' Tales from the Jersey Shore 1764-1955* — "As fresh as a sea breeze," said *Library Journal.*
- *Josephine: From Washington Working Girl to Fisherman's Wife* — The true story of a 20th century woman ahead of her time.
- *Fisherman's Wife* — Beautifully illustrated by LBI artist **Julie Goldstein**, a moving true story of love and adversity on LBI during the Great Depression.

The Oyster Singer — columnist and author **Larry Savadove**'s novel captures a delightful authentic local culture with colorful characters escaping a changing LBI.

Great Storms of the Jersey Shore, by **Larry Savadove**, **Margaret Thomas Buchholz**, and **Scott Mazzella** — "one of the best documented compendiums" of coastal storms, according to *The New York Times*. In stories and pictures it explores wild weather from the first recorded Jersey Shore storms through Superstorm Sandy.

A disappearing South Jersey bay and pinelands culture and lifestyle, rarely seen by visitors, is shared in *The Bayman: A Life on Barnegat Bay*, by **Merce Ridgway**.

Surviving Sandy: Long Beach Island and the Greatest Storm of the Jersey Shore, by **Scott Mazzella**, documents, with personal accounts and photographs, the remarkable experiences and resilience of the LBI community in the worst storm in generations.

Tales From An Endless Summer — **Bruce Novotny**'s lyrical coming-of-age surf novel, set in a 1980s Long Beach Island summer, continues to ring true.

Four Seasons At the Shore — This oversize art hardcover with hundreds of photographs and scores of contributors favors LBI. Island writers **Larry Savadove, Sandy Gingras,** and **Margaret Thomas** share evocative seasonal essays.

Local Color: Long Beach Island's Photographic History Reimagined by **Leslee Ganss** and **Ray Fisk** offers a uniquely different look at the island's past with beautifully hand-colored historic photographs paired with historic details. Vibrant new life is breathed into moments, stories, and lost landmarks in a book that blurs the lines between a delightful gallery exhibition, a fine art coffee-table book, and a history.

Sandy Gingras, award-winning author and poet. Her first book, *How To Live on An Island,* was followed by *How To Live At the Beach, Reasons To Be Happy at the Beach, In A House By The Sea* (all inspired by LBI), and many other titles sold nationally. *I Love You Long Beach Island*, conceived during Superstorm Sandy, celebrates the fragility, beauty, and strength of this island.

Gretchen Coyle and **Deb Whitcraft's** *Tucker's Island* explores in pictures and text the lost community south of Holgate. Their large-format *Inferno At Sea*, about the Morro Castle disaster at Asbury Park, is a worthy companion to the largest collection of Morro Castle items at the Maritime Museum in Beach Haven.

Corinne G. Ruff's *Island Child: Life Lessons From the Shore,* illustrated by **Lisa Benjamin**, shares resident's and visitor's delights and philosophy inspired by LBI.

Stafford Chronicles (by the staff of *The SandPaper*) profiles many of the figures whose lives left a mark on LBI and explores the shared history of mainland and island.

Fascinating historical accounts from the Island, the Shore, and the entire state can be found in *New Jersey In History: Fighting to be Heard*, by **Thomas Farner**.

Too Many Summers, by **L. Ganss,** a collection of three decades of LBI-centric cartoons from *The SandPaper,* captures the rituals, delights, irony and eccentricities of life on this island in all seasons.

All *Your* Things LBI

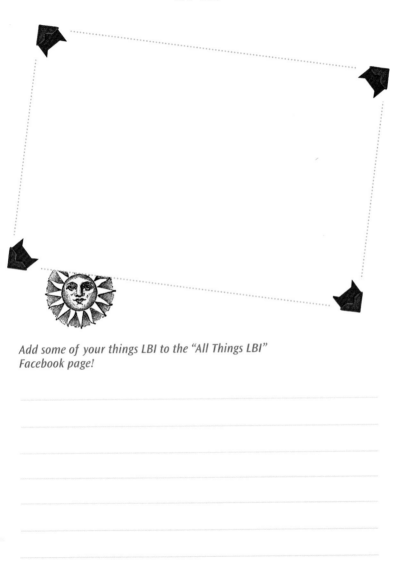

Add some of your things LBI to the "All Things LBI"
Facebook page!

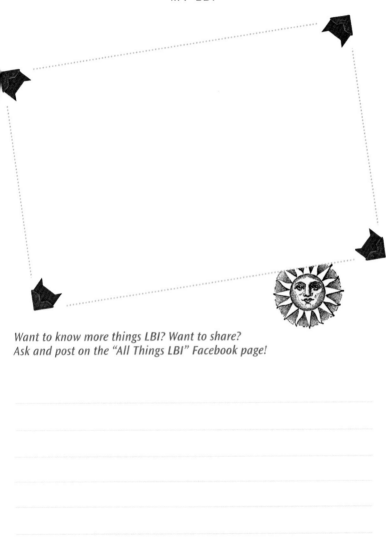

Want to know more things LBI? Want to share?
Ask and post on the "All Things LBI" Facebook page!

We've been making original books, calendars, cards and historical videos about LBI (and the rest of the Shore — as well as New Jersey) since 1984. No cookie-cutter formula, every project is created and designed from the ground up. Small-batch, local publishing!

Check out all our titles:
down-the-shore.com

*Want to know more things LBI? Want to share?
Join the "All Things LBI" Facebook group!*